CANNY HISTO

CARLISLE

JIM ELDRIDGE

BOOKCASE

ISBN1904147135
First edition: 2006.
Copyright: Jim Eldridge, 2006.
Published by Bookcase
19 Castle Street, Carlisle, CA3 8SY
01228 544560   bookcasecarlisle@aol.co

CONTENTS

Here I am at the heart of Carlisle, sitting on the steps of the Old Carel Cross in front of the Town Hall.

INTRODUCTION

There are some history books that are so full of scholarship and academic brilliance that you feel humble even as you open the first page and gaze in reverence on the magnificent intellect that must have produced it.

This isn't one of those books.

This is a book by an off-comer, an incomer, a blow-in, one who moved to north Cumbria some years ago and settled here, and loves it, and intends to make it his last resting place (but not, I hope, too quickly). The dates in it (of which there are quite a few) are accurate, as are the facts presented. However, there are some flights of imagination among them. But then Cumbria has always been a place of myths, legends and stories.

In the beginning, saith the prophet, was the word, and in this case the word is . . . Carlisle.

But what does "Carlisle" mean? Where does it come from? I have heard various suggestions: that it is a corruption of the family name Carlyle; or that it comes from the fact that this was a place where, in ancient times, carts were parked on an island on a meeting point of two rivers, the Esk and the Eden (cart-isle).

In fact, the name means "The Camp of Lug". It's Celtic Irish with additions by the Romans, reworked by the Welsh Britons, and then mis-spelt to the Normans. Confused? Understandably.

When the Romans first arrived, the area had already been settled by the Celtic Brigante tribe. One of the major Celtic Gods (in Irish Celtic mythology) was called Lug. The ancient festival of Lughanasa is named after him. As the British Celts were the same race as the Irish Celts, spoke the same language, and kept in touch with each other across the Irish Sea, it is quite likely they worshipped the same Gods, including Lug.

The Romans were dab hands at incorporating local interests wherever they conquered as a way of keeping the chances of rebellion down, and they had already had trouble with the Brigantes rebelling, so the Romans called the fort they built in the area "Lugavalium". In Latin, this either meant "The Oak of Lug", or "Lug's Place" or "The Place Where Lug Took Tablets To Ease Stress and Tension."

When the Romans left some 300 years later, the name reverted to its Celtic form, only by this time the dominant form of Celtic was Welsh. (This was because Wales, along with Cornwall and Scotland, was a part of Britain the Romans hadn't been able to conquer, and so the Celtic tradition had flourished there). So the name became "Caer Lug" (Celtic Welsh for "camp or fort of Lug"). However, the Welsh have never been content with using just one "L" where two will do, and so it became "Caer-Llug", which soon became (for reasons of pronunciation in Celtic Welsh) "Caer-Lluel".

The Normans, who arrived in this area in 1092, were great ones for producing lists of the places they owned, so the King could make sure he got the right amount of taxes. It is quite likely that the Norman official who was preparing the list for this area asked a local Celt (or a Saxon or Viking, because by then the area was full of those as well): "What do you call this place?" and the local replied "Caer-Lluel". To which the Norman would have said: "How do you spell that?" And the local would have said: "I'm sorry, I don't read or write."

The Norman, who spoke French, would have asked the local to repeat the name "Caer-Lluel", and then tried to write it down as he heard it: "The first part sounds like Car ... and the second part sounds like ... um ... l'ile (French for island)". And he would have written down "Carlile". He would then have shown it to the local, who (unable to read) would have nodded and said, "That looks right to me."

Later someone would have corrected his spelling and pointed out that in the English version of "island" there was an "s", and so it became "Carlisle".

So there we have it. Carlisle got its name because of various spelling mistakes.. But then, good spelling has always been regarded with suspicion by most people .. something akin to witchcraft, as if there's something supernatural about people who can spell properly. Even Shakespeare had different ways of spelling his name, which must have caused great confusion among the autograph collectors hanging around the Globe Theatre in Sixteenth Century London:

"This is William Shakespeare's autograph!"

"No, this is!"

"Are you calling me a liar!" .. etc etc.

But all this talk of Normans and Welsh Britons is getting ahead of ourselves. We need to go back to the beginning . . . .

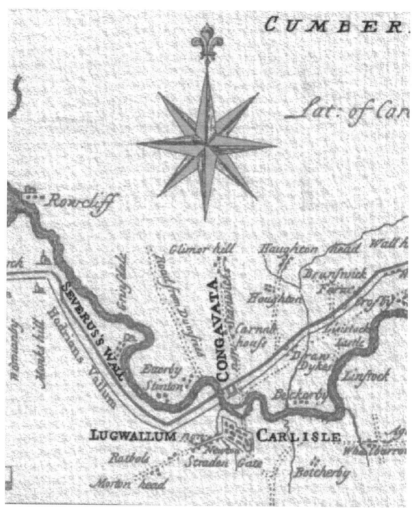

A section from John Warburton's map of Hadrian's Wall, which he drew in 1753. It shows the line of the Wall crossing the Eden just north of the Castle and then going out along the Solway. On this map the Wall is named after the Emperor Severus and Hadrian is credited with building the Vallum or ditch.

Above left: A Roman stone from Tullie House.

8

1 - EARLY DAYS - THE ROMANS

There were people in the area which became Carlisle during the Middle Stone Age, about 4,000 years BC, who had chosen to settle in this wet and marshy landscape, at a place where two rivers (later called the Caldew and the Petteril) ran into the larger River Eden.

During Neolithic times (the New Stone Age) new arrivals came, bringing with them such new-fangled devices as stone axes and other tools with which they cleared the land.

They were followed over a lengthy period of time by Bronze Age and Iron Age people, and then Celts. All of these took one look at the landscape and decided it was so inhospitable and wet that no-one in their right mind would want to settle here, which meant there was very little chance of some other rival tribe coming and stealing their land or arriving

9

Some of the old Roman remains in the garden of Tullie House

and conquering them. (Before I get letters of complaint from Cumbrians who think I may be slandering the fair county by describing it as particularly wet just because it rains a lot of the time now, and would protest that in days gone by Cumbria was one of the sunniest spots on the planet and akin to St Tropez before Global Warming and Climate Change kicked in . . . meteorologists who have studied the weather in ancient times have asserted that in the late Bronze Age and the Iron Age, extreme winds from the west made the landscape of what was to become Cumbria wetter than it had been during the previous 2000 years. And it's been raining here ever since.)

This theory that the Cumbrian landscape was too forbidding for anyone to consider conquering it worked well until AD72, when the Romans arrived.

The Romans had actually been in the more southerly parts of Britain for some time. Julius Caesar had first arrived with his army in southern Britain in 55 BC, but after declaring Britain part of the Roman Empire, the Romans left and forgot about it for the next 97 years until the

Emperor Claudius sent his troops to reconquer it in AD43. It was almost another 30 years before the Romans decided to venture to the far north of Cumbria. Their reason for coming this far north was to quell the tribe of the Brigantes, who lived in this northern region, and who had risen up in revolt against the Romans in AD69.

During the winter of AD72 and AD73, the Romans built the first fort at Carlisle, made of timber and turf. The Roman Governor of Britain at that time was Petillius Cerialis, who was also the son-in-law of the Emperor, Vaspasian, proving the old-adage: the son-in-law also rises. As we have seen, the Romans called this place Lugavalium.

The Romans used the fort at Carlisle as the base for attacks on the tribes of Scotland, who they tried to subdue and bring under Roman control, but ten years of fighting (and being defeated by) the Scots led the Romans to decide: If at first you don't succeed ... give up. Following the decisive battle of Mons Graupius in Scotland in AD83, the Romans withdrew to Carlisle and proceeded to strengthen their fort there.

The Romans are remembered for introducing many things to Britain: central heating, the calendar, sanitation, straight roads, cabbages, carrots, wigs, false teeth, stinging nettles, etc etc . . . but in the Carlisle area the most famous thing they established was The Wall. Better known as Hadrian's Wall, which was begun in AD122.

Hadrian's Wall was a direct result of the Roman's failure to defeat the Scots. Aware that the Scots had given them a thrashing in Scotland and might come into England and do the same thing there, the Romans decided to build a wall to keep them out.

(There was another later Wall built east-west across Britain by another Roman emperor, the Emperor Antonine. This one was in Scotland, and was begun in AD143, but is not nearly so famous. In fact, most people have never even heard of it.)

Carlisle developed as a Roman town. Remains of major Roman building and trinkets and other artefacts have been discovered on the site of what is now The Lanes Shopping Centre, and also Blackfriars Street.

The largest fort on Hadrian's Wall was built at Stanwix, in the north of Carlisle. It covered an area of 9.5 acres, and one of the Romans' top cavalry regiments, consisting of 1,000 men (and, of, course, their horses), was stationed here; the largest cavalry unit in the whole of Britain. The importance of Stanwix can further be seen in the fact that the Senior Commander of the whole Wall garrison lived at the Stanwix fort.

Any permanent military garrison attracts merchants and traders, and Carlisle was no exception. Roman remains found in Blackfriars Street included brooches, pottery, glass beads, and also some very expensive items such as glass jugs and cups.

Now either the Roman soldier was a lot more sophisticated than we had previously been led to believe, and used to sit around after a hard day's marching and fighting, supping fine wines from glass goblets with his fellow soldiers . . . .

"I say, Marcus Antonius, this wine from Gaul is rather fine. An unpretentious and amusing red but with an interesting aftertaste of horse."

"That would be the smell from the stables. Personally, I prefer this heaving mass of brown ale with a thick white head on it from Newcastle."

Or . . . over the many years the Romans were at Carlisle, some of the soldiers married local women, retired, raised families, and sat around as civilians in their centrally heated conservatories, admiring their plumbing, sipping wine and dreaming of the day that someone would invent golf.

One thing we know for sure: during the years of Roman occupation, Carlisle grew in size. By the time the Romans abandoned Lugavalium as a military garrison, it was a large and thriving city. The fact that the Romans abandoned Lugavalium does not mean they disappeared. Many Roman soldiers settled here and had families. Mixing with the local Celts, they became known as Romano-British. And one of the most famous Romano-Britons was none other than King Arthur.

2 - KING ARTHUR AND THE CELTS, AND THE SAXONS

King Arthur was the Celtic equivalent of Elvis Presley. In both cases, the King has been sighted everywhere. Arthur is reported to have fought battles in Wales, Cornwall, Eastern England, and the Carlisle area. The evidence for Arthur having been in Cumbria are the village of Arthuret (Arthur is said to be buried in the church there), and "Arthur's Round Table" near Penrith. Scant and circumstantial evidence maybe, but people have been hanged on far less.

What written evidence there is, mainly from monks such as Gildas and Nennius, suggest that Arthur was actually a Romano-Briton known as Ambrosius Aurelianus. After the Roman military machine had finally left

Above: King Arthur entering Carlisle from the book of the Historical Pageant staged in Carlisle in 1951.

An old legend tells of St Cuthbert visiting the city in 685 and causing water to flow from an old Roman fountain. This illustration from a 12th century manuscript shows St. Cuthbert with his staff and the water flowing from the fountain like a snake out of a sack. In the Cathedral there are a series of medieval pictures telling the story of the life of St Cuthbert.

Britain in the Fifth Century, Ambrosius led a troop of mounted warriors defending Britain against the invading Saxons. Why or how this Ambrosius Aurelianus changed his name to Arthur; or whether the local Britons took to calling him "Arthur" because it was easier to say, or whether this was the same "Arthur" who pops up at Tintagel and in Somerset and all over Wales is not known.

One thing that is known is that the Celtic/Romano-British resistance against the Saxons was ultimately not very successful, because from about AD540 until 1092, all the rulers of this area have definitely Saxon-sounding names, such as Ethelfrith, Eanfrith, Aldfrith, Coelwulf, Ethelred and Egbert.

Even if there are doubts about Arthur (aka Ambrosius) being in this area, it is a fact that there were some famous people of the time who were at Carlisle. Whether they were resident or whether they passing through to somewhere else, it is not clear, as these were known as The Dark Ages, and things weren't written down as much as had been the case under the Romans. Consequently, Visitors Books didn't get filled in very often.

One person who definitely was in the Carlisle area was St Patrick. We know this from a letter he wrote in which he says that his grandfather was a priest at a church in the area, and his father was a deacon at the same church. As this is the same Patrick who became a Saint, and also saved Ireland from being infested with snakes, it is safe to assume he was being honest about this, and not just boasting.

Another famous person of the time was Urien, King of Rheged, whose Kingdom included the lands around the Solway Firth, which included Carlisle. However, whether he spent much time here is unknown. He may have popped in now and then to see how things were going, collect a few taxes and execute a few people, the sort of everyday thing that Celtic Kings of the time did.

Actually, Carlisle in the Sixth and Seventh Centuries was quite a place for Celtic Saints. As well as the aforementioned St Patrick there was also St Kentigern (one of King Urien's sons), and St Cuthbert (Bishop of Lindisfarne) and St Herbert (who became a hermit on the island in Derwentwater, on what is know as Herbert's Island). One can imagine a whole bunch of Saints meeting up in the Saints Arms after a hard day's missionary work and moaning about how hard it was to convert the ordinary Cumbrians to Christianity.

"How's the missionary work in Carlisle going, Herbert?"

"An absolute waste of time, Cuthbert. All the locals want to do is watch some game where eleven men on each side kick a pig's bladder around a field and try and get it through a pair of tall sticks set up at each end."

"Oh? What's the game called?"

"Cricket."

Unlike Roman times, which has lots of dates (e.g. 55BC, AD122, etc), there are very few memorable dates in Cumbria during the times of the Celts and the Saxons. The only one we know for certain is AD685, and concerns a Saint (naturally): in this case Saint Cuthbert, Bishop of

Lindisfarne. St Cuthbert arrived in Carlisle to meet the Queen of Northumbria, who was waiting for news of her husband, King Ecgfrith. We do not know the exact nature of the news that Cuthbert brought her, but as King Ecgfrith died in 685, we can assume it was not good news. While he was in Carlisle giving the queen the not very good news, St Cuthbert took the time to found a monastery, which was named after him. This monastery is believed to have been in the area where St Cuthbert's Church and the Cathedral now stand.

3 - THE VIKINGS

The Vikings (or Danes) came to Carlisle in 876. They announced their arrival by doing what Vikings did best, which was to sack, lay waste and generally destroy the area with fire and sword. According to John of Worcester, Carlisle was "deserted for two hundred years after the attack" ... although this does sound a bit like exaggeration. However, after the Vikings arrived there was even less history recorded than there had been during the time of the Saxons.

We know the Vikings were here (even if no-one else was, having run away in fear) from archaeological finds: a bone comb and a penny from the reign of King Edgar were found during a dig at Tullie House; a bead was uncovered at Scotch Street, and a disc brooch was uncovered at Old Grapes Lane. Not as much as has been found when compared to Roman remains, but considering that the Vikings tended to destroy

Above: Men upto their waists in the waters of the Solway still fishing with haaf nets as the Vikings used to do.

17

Archaeologists digging in the Cathedral grounds in 1988. Carlisle was thought to have been deserted in Viking times, but there had been 40 Viking burials on this one site alone. Carlisle was obviously inhabited during these years.

everything, it is amazing anything was found at all.

The Vikings were not newcomers to Britain. They had been making raids on the land since at least 789, and by 830 these raids had become an annual event. All attempts by the Saxons to defend against these raids failed, and finally in 876 a kind of truce was reached at Wedmore in Somerset in which Britain was carved up between the Saxons and the Vikings. A line was drawn from London to Chester: south of that line was Saxon territory, and the Vikings would keep to the north of the line. This was known as "Danelaw". However, many Saxons in the north did not think much of this idea and continued to fight back against the Viking raids for many years after Danelaw was established. When the Saxons couldn't fight back, they tried to buy off the Vikings. The Vikings took the money and went away, and then returned and attacked northern Britain later.

In 1013 the Viking Sweyn Forkbeard defeated the Saxon King Ethelred II (aka Ethelred the Unready) and declared himself King of Denmark, Norway and all of England. However, after Sweyn's death in 1014 there was a major struggle for the throne of England between the Saxon Edmund II, the son of Ethelred, and Sweyn's son, Cnut. In 1016 Cnut and Edmund reached an agreement: they would partition the country and rule their own separate areas, and the one who lived longest would then take over the kingship of the whole country. Unfortunately for

18

Edmund, he died a few weeks after this agreement was reached, and Cnut became the overall king of England.

One major impact of the Vikings in the area around Carlisle is in place names: all place names ending in "-by" are Viking in origin: Harraby, Botcherby, Wetherby; Oughterby, Scotby, Aglionby, Longsowerby, Thursby, etc.

One other thing the Vikings did bring to this area was haaf-netting.

Haaf-netting is a type of fishing carried out in the Solway Firth to the west of Carlisle. From June 1st to 9th September, you may see men, in lines or singly, standing sometimes chest-deep in the Solway Firth at the turn of the tides at Bowness-on-Solway, holding large wooden netted frames. They are the haaf-netters. The word "haaf" is an old Norse word meaning "channel". The haaf-net itself is a wooden frame (also called "the beam") 5.5m long by 2.2m high, from which a net is suspended. It is said that the beam is the exact length of a Viking oar, without the blade.

The usual method of fishing is for a line of fishermen, each with a haaf-net, to form a line across the channels of the Solway at low tide, though some fishermen also fish alone. The two main fish caught using this method are Atlantic Salmon and Sea Trout.

It is a very hard (and sometimes dangerous) way to catch fish, and the Vikings would be very proud of the fact that it still continues. Valhalla lives on the Solway Firth!

Standing in front of the Norman keep of the castle.

4 - THE NORMANS

It is often said that there is one date in English history that everyone remembers: 1066: the Norman Invasion. For Carlisle, this Norman Invasion actually happened some 26 years later, in 1092, but then north Cumbria has always been a little behind in some things.

In 1092 William Rufus (son of William the Conqueror) set off to check this most northern part of his kingdom. Whether it really was part of his kingdom is open to debate, because in 945 Cumberland had been granted to King Malcolm of Scotland by King Edmund of England. It is worth pointing out that north Cumberland does not figure in the

Above: The City Charter from 1353, issued by Edward III. Earlier charters had been destroyed in fires.

21

Domesday Book, because the officials sent out by William the Conqueror in 1086 to list everywhere in his newly conquered land obviously believed the locals when they told them that north Cumberland was part of Scotland, and pointed out that places in North Cumbria had names such as Kirkbampton, Kirkbride, Kirkandrews-on-Eden - all very Scottish sounding places. William I's officials duly returned to London and told their King that although south Cumberland was his (and proved it by listing Millom, Whicham, Kirksanton and Bootle), north Cumberland wasn't.

William's son, William Rufus, however, thought he'd check for himself, and when he arrived in Carlisle he found it full of Saxons, Vikings and Scots, with a few remaining Celts clinging grimly on. Despite supposedly being part of Scotland, the Carlisle area was ruled over by one Dolfin, a Saxon. In true Norman fashion, William Rufus kicked Dolfin out and took the town over himself, claiming Cumberland as part of England.

The Scottish King at this time was Malcom III, and he must have been fairly miffed to lose this part of his Kingdom, handed down through generations, but as a Saxon had actually been lording over Carlisle at the time, and as the Normans had changed all the rules and cancelled all previous Treaties, Gifts, etc, when they arrived in 1066, there wasn't a lot Malcolm III could do about it except sulk.

One of the first things the Normans did when they took over anywhere was build a castle on high ground from which they could control the surrounding area, and Carlisle was no exception. William Rufus's castle which was made of timber on earth mounds is not the Castle we see today, but it certainly set the foundations for it.

William also set about carving Cumberland up into different Baronies, which he handed out to his cronies. Ranulf le Meschin was given the lordship of Carlisle, and other lordships were created for Normans such as Gille son of Buet (Gilsland), Richard le Rydere (Rickerby), Guerri the Fleming (Werryholme, now called Willowholme) among others.

When William Rufus died, his younger brother Henry became King Henry I. Henry I came to Carlisle in 1122 and decided that the place needed an even bigger castle, one that actually looked like a castle, with proper towers and battlements, a stone keep and city walls spreading out from it.

Henry - aware that all Kings died sooner or later - was also very keen to gain Brownie Points in Heaven when he got there, and so he set about making sure that Carlisle was known to be a Holy Place, and that he - Henry - had done it. He appointed his personal confessor, Aethewulf, as the first Bishop of Carlisle in 1133.

We can only hope that this paid off and when he got to Heavenly Gates, Henry was made welcome, because it happened sooner than he might have expected. In 1135 Henry I died as a result of, it is said, "a surfeit of lampreys". Lampreys are eel-like creatures. Apparently his doctor had warned him against eating them, but some eating habits die hard. Possibly Henry thought that by turning Carlisle into a Godly Place he would get away with eating a plateful of lampreys without getting indigestion. He was wrong.

The period after Henry's death bought chaos to England, especially as to who was to replace him as ruler. Carlisle, being on the border between England and Scotland, was to suffer special confusion in this time.

After Henry I died there were a whole heap of people all claiming that they were the rightful heir to the throne of England. The major contenders were Stephen, the Count of Blois and his wife, Adela (she being the daughter of William I); and Matilda, daughter of Henry I and Matilda of Scotland and also niece of Stephen and Adela. This proves once again that every family has trouble with its relations.

King David of Scotland was quick to leap into the fray, throwing his hat into the ring on behalf of Matilda, and claiming Carlisle and the surrounding areas of Cumberland and Westmoreland as his part of the bargain. It could be said that David had a further valid claim to the lands: he was a Prince of Cumbria. He was considered to be one of the most powerful English barons, as well as King of the Scots..

Because Stephen had enough on his plate with trying to fight a series of battles with Matilda's army, Stephen let David have Carlisle and the surrounding area. And so Carlisle became a Scottish city.

After a see-saw of Royalty in England between the two rivals, with each being appointed Ruler and then deposed, Stephen was finally crowned King in 1141. However, when Stephen died in 1154, it was Matilda's son, another Henry (Henry II) who became King of England.

One of the first things Henry did was demand Carlisle and Cumberland and Westmorland back from the Scots. King David had died in Carlisle Castle the year before, in 1153, at the age of 69, a venerable age for that time. The new Scottish King, Malcolm IV (who was only eleven years old when he came to the throne) obviously decided this new English King was bigger and tougher than him, as well as being taller and older. And so Carlisle was returned to England.

Poor Malcolm had a terrible reign as King of Scotland. Not only did Henry II take Carlisle back for England, but the King of Norway turned up and sacked Aberdeen, and a group of rebel Scottish Lords under the leadership of Somerled, the ancestor of the Macdonald Lord of the Isles, took the opportunity to lay waste to Glasgow. Twelve years after taking on the throne of Scotland, at the age of 24, defeated, unmarried and fed up, Malcolm died in 1165.

His brother who took over the throne, William the Lion, was a different kettle of fish altogether. Tough, fierce, and - above all - determined to get Carlisle back into Scottish territory.

In 1173, William saw an opportunity: Henry II's eldest son, also called Henry, had launched a rebellion against his father. With both Henrys engaged in knocking bits out of each other, it was a good time to strike. William sent a message to Henry II saying that unless Carlisle and the surrounding territories were restored to Scotland he would no longer recognise Henry as King of England and pay homage to him. Henry apparently took time out from battling with his eldest son to send a reply to William to the effect of "Oh yeah!", accompanied by a drawing of two fingers.

So, in 1173 William the Lion crossed the border and laid siege to Carlisle. However, on hearing that Henry (the King, not his son) was sending a large force north to defend Carlisle, William withdrew back across the border, and waited until these reinforcements had been recalled south.

Henry recalled his troops back to the south of England to continue battles there, and once again William the Lion launched an attack on Carlisle.

By now it was a year further on, 1174.

This time William had enlarged his force to 80,000 men, just in case Henry II's army came back. For three months the Scots laid siege to

Carlisle, but the garrison in the Castle, led by the Governor of Carlisle, Robert de Vaux, held out against them. However, after three months of siege things inside the Castle were looking grim: food was in short supply, and Robert de Vaux and his men agreed that they might as well surrender before they were forced to eat one another. But just as they were about to run up the white flag, a most amazing thing happened: William snatched defeat from the jaws of victory by being captured at Alnwick on 13 July 1174 by Henry II's forces, who had obviously sneaked up on him when he wasn't looking.

Without their King, the Scots couldn't see much point in carrying on with the siege, so they returned back across the border to Scotland to moan about the price of haggis. William the Lion, meanwhile, was forced to sign a treaty (the Treaty of Falaise) saying he would keep the peace and not keep attacking England, especially the bits of it that included Carlisle. Although William signed this treaty, he obviously kept his fingers crossed while doing it, because he appeared to have told his son, Alexander, "Carlisle is rightfully ours. When I'm dead and gone, see that you get it back."

William died in 1214. Two years later his son, now Alexander II of Scotland, launched an attack against Carlisle. At the time he took over as King of Scotland, Alexander was just sixteen years of age . . . not old enough to vote (if there had been such a thing as the voter at that time), but old enough to run the country.

Henry II was not a man who had a lot of luck with his four sons. Nowadays we would say they had a severely dysfunctional relationship.

Henry (the King's eldest son) had been offered support by his younger brother, Geoffrey, if Henry wanted to attack any other member of his family: father, brothers, cousins, etc. Doubtless Geoffrey, as the third brother (and also known as a "natural son" i.e. illegitimate), had worked out that he had to bump off at least two of his brothers if he had any hope of being King, and perhaps thought that if he could persuade brother Henry to have an all-out fight with brother Richard, there was a very good chance that his two older brothers might kill themselves, and hopefully kill his younger brother John while they were doing it.

In the event, following the unsuccessful rebellion of 1173-74, Henry (the son) died of dysentery in June 1183.

King Henry II died in 1189 and was succeeded by his son Richard (aka "The Lionheart").

At this point poor Geoffrey must have lost heart with this whole business of getting to be King, so he went off and joined the Church, and became Archbishop of York.

When Richard died in 1199, he was succeeded by King John, who was King of England at the time. Alexander launched his attack against Carlisle. This was very lucky indeed for Alexander, because King John was one of the most despised and hated Kings and most of the English Barons were in rebellion against him.

John had visited Carlisle four times during his reign, and each time he came it was to announce yet another tax. Politicians take note: this did not endear him to the population.

When Alexander arrived at Carlisle in 1216, promising to overthrow the rule of the English King in the area, the people of the city - fed up with King John and his taxes - were keen to welcome the young Scottish King and his army in, as were the Prior and convent of Carlisle, who considered that "King John had done them many injuries". The only dissenting voiced was that of Robert de Vieuxpont, who had been appointed by King John to defend Carlisle against the Scots and was determined to carry out his King's orders. However, soon after, King John died, and Robert de Vieuxpont obviously decided that defending a dead King was not very sensible, and so the gates of Carlisle were opened and Alexander took control of the city without a battle.

Henry III (John's son, who took over the English throne after his father died) was not going to let Carlisle go so easily. Or, rather, his advisers weren't, because at the time he became King, Henry III was just nine year old. There followed years of disputes about whether Carlisle belonged to Scotland or England, until finally the border between the two countries was defined at the Treaty of York in 1237.

Carlisle was now definitely part of England. (Except as far as the Scots were concerned).

While all this politics and to-and-froing was going on about whether Carlisle was Scottish or English, and who should be King of England or Scotland, the people of Carlisle were glad that sieges and wars were over (at least, for the moment) and could go about their business.

And what business it was.

Events during the later part of the Thirteenth Century read like a page from an early version of "The Cumberland News", with stories of drunkenness, murder and mayhem, domestic turbulence, and major destruction.

In 1251 most of Carlisle was destroyed by fire. The Rickergate was destroyed, as was much of the eastern part of the city, including the Moot Hall, in which were kept the city's charters. The King responded by giving 200 oaks from the Royal forest at Inglewood to the people of Carlisle to enable them to rebuild their homes.

In 1287, a certain Ralph Deblet, after having had too much to drink, staggered and crawled upstairs to go to bed. Unfortunately, the bed he fell on was already occupied by one Thomas Tailor. Poor Thomas woke up, shocked at suddenly finding this man dropping on him, and possibly fearing the worst, threw Ralph off him.

Ralph, equally shocked, fell backwards, and tumbled down the stairs he had just crawled up. Sadly for Ralph, instead of landing in a bruised heap at the bottom of the stairs, and then crawling away to sleep it off somewhere else, he landed on a cartload of wood and died.

Thomas, for his part, was found guilty of murder and hanged.

In 1292 it is recorded that Richard Clement hit the dog of Roger, son of Martin the butcher. Roger reacted by thrusting his sword through Richard's heart, killing him.

Also in 1292 a young man called Simon of Orton, angry because his father had disinherited him, set fire to his family's house. Unfortunately it didn't occur to Simon that setting fire to a house in a town built mainly of wood (see: the rebuilding of Carlisle with oaks from Inglewood in 1251, above) was not the brightest of ideas, but even today most vandals lack what could be termed intelligence or forethought.

The result was a catastrophic fire which spread through Carlisle, burning the cathedral, the friaries, the bridge of the castle, and many buildings. Nine people died. Simon was sentenced to be burnt for committing arson, and also to be hanged for murder. Though whether he was burnt first and then hung afterwards, or hung first and then burnt, or whether both executions were carried out simultaneously and he was hung with a rope which was set on fire, it is not known.

The gateway into the Castle as it is today. The castleyard is now a car park and the battlements overlook a congested dual carriageway which cuts the Castle off from its city.

5 - THE CASTLE

The spot where Carlisle Castle stands, high on a bluff overlooking the meandering River Eden, along with its tributaries the Petterill and the Caldew, is the perfect place for a military fortification. The Romans spotted that at once when they arrived in the area in AD72.

During the first winter the Romans were here (AD72-73) they set to work building a fort made of timber and turf to protect their garrison against attacks by rebelling Brigantes (the Celtic tribe who lived in the area) and the Scots.

During the hundreds of years the Romans were here, a large town developed around the fort.

In 1092, William Rufus, the son of William the Conqueror, arrived in the area and decided the existing fort wasn't up to Norman standards, and set about building one that was. However, at this stage there was no thought of using large amounts of masonry: William Rufus's new fort was still to be built mainly of wood. This was understandable as most of the people in the area who seemed to pose the most threat did not possess very

Above: Carlisle Castle was built on the site of an earlier Roman fort by William Rufus (son of William the Conqueror) in 1092, but began to take the shape we recognise today when William Rufus's brother, Henry I, started construction of a fully fortified Castle in 1122.

large weapons: mainly bows and arrows and swords, and William Rufus must have felt that a wooden fort would be strong enough to deal with those.

However, when William died his younger brother, Henry I became King of England, and Henry was the kind of King who felt that a Castle had to look like a proper Castle if it was going to intimidate people and stop them attacking it. So when Henry came to Carlisle in 1122 and saw the existing wooden fort, he must have sniffed in a superior way, and said, "Not bad for a holiday chalet, but not my idea of a Castle!" and then set about turning Carlisle Castle into a Properly Fortified Castle made of stone.

To carve the local red sandstone into blocks, Henry brought Flemish and Norman masons over from the Continent. These masons had many years experience at building Norman castles and knew what they were doing, and how to do it quickly. It is possible that Henry tried using local Cumbrian stonemasons at first, but would have got impatient with the fact that the Cumbrians would have preferred to carve stone in their own style (irregular but interesting shapes, adorned with Celtic patterns, fascinating to look at but difficult to build a castle with) and also they kept stopping for lunch breaks.

The most famous of these stonemasons was a Fleming called Botchardus. The area of Carlisle called Botcherby was named after him. Language historians will note that local sensitivities were thought of in naming the area after this Fleming, by adding the Danish (or Viking) -by after the first part of Botchardus's name. All local names of places that end with -by (Rickerby, Harraby,Etterby, etc) show this Viking influence. I suppose it can be seen as an early example of political correctness, keeping the local Vikings happy.

With the influx of the large number of Fleming and Norman masons needed to build the castle, many of whom brought their families with them, there was an awareness that there could be trouble between the new immigrants and the existing populations, a mixture of Celts, Saxons, Scots and Vikings. As a result, the city was divided into three main areas: one for the Normans and Flemings, one for the Saxons, and one for the Scots. The Celts were left to camp outside.

It is at this point that linguistic and national confusion kicks in:

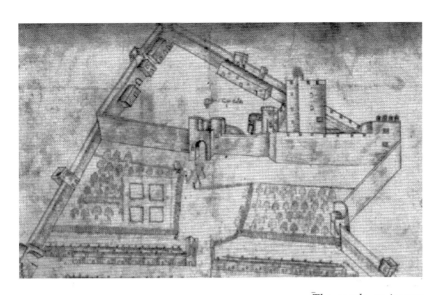

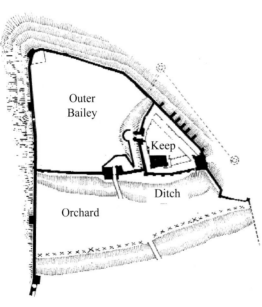

The castle as it was drawn on a map of Carlisle in 1560. The tall keep dominated both the castle and the city. There were two ditches and a stockade between the castle and the city and at one time there was a moat between the inner and outer bailey.

Outer Bailey

Keep

Ditch

Orchard

The Castle from the Lady's Walk in an engraving by Nutter.

Because many of the Scots had originally come from Ireland, the Normans described them as Irish. And as the Saxons had arrived on their initial conquest with the Angles (or English), they were called English. And so, in theory, we have three areas of the city, each with its own gate: one for the Scots (aka the Irish = Irishgate)); one for the Saxons (aka the English = English Gate) and the Flemings - led by Botchardus - living in the area near the Botchard gate.

However, according to a sixteenth century history of Carlisle and its gates, the following was the reality:

The Scotch Gate (previously known as The Richard Gate, because it led to the lands of Richard le Rydere, and later called Rickergate) was in the North Walls.

The Irish Gate (also known as the Caldew Gate) was to the west of the city.

The English Gate was also known as the Botchard Gate and was to the south of the city. However, the same historian goes on to say:

The English families were placed near both the Richard Gate (aka the Scottish Gate) and Botchard Gate.

The Irish families were placed in Abbey Street.

The Flemings and Normans lived in Castle Street.

But back to the construction of the Castle: although most of the masonry is of the red sandstone found in the area, the foundations were made from grey sandstone. The construction of the early part of the Castle is very similar to the construction of the Cathedral, which was being built at the same time. Henry's imported masons were obviously kept very busy, working on the Castle and the Cathedral at the same time.

Not that the Fleming masons cut every piece of stone. They also kept up the local tradition of recycling that had been carried out once the Romans had left.

Visitors to this area often comment on the lack of any actual visible remains of Hadrian's Wall. They are quite wrong, the remains of the Wall are all around them, only they have been incorporated into local buildings. When the Romans left, the local people simply stole The Wall. They

The inner gate

33

dismantled it and built their own houses out of it.

Roman stone can be identified by the way it is dressed *(a very impressive technical word which means the way it is shaped and cut)*, because the Roman masons used a "diamond brooch" style of cutting. Prime examples of this type of stone dressing can be found in the Cumbrian village where I live, where many of the houses and the local Church are made from stones that all show this Roman style of cutting and shaping. In the same way, the Flemish masons found perfectly good blocks of stone lying around from Roman times, and saved themselves a lot of time and trouble by putting those into the building of the Castle.

The Castle itself is of the traditional Norman motte-and-bailey style: an outer bailey and an inner ward. The outer walls of the Castle extended almost to the City walls, but with a deliberate gap between the Castle and the City, consisting of a ditch. This made sure there could be no sudden surprise attacks on the Castle from the City.

In 1124 Henry I died, and in the confusion that followed as different factions fought for the throne of England, King David I of Scotland claimed Carlisle for Scotland.

David I strengthened the Castle by increasing the height of the Walls, and had more inner and outer wards constructed, and more ditches, although it has been suggested that all these additions were made from wood and not stone.

It is also recorded that it was during David I's reign that the city walls were built, although the suggestion, again, is that these walls were made of timber and not stone. As there is a record of the gates to the city existing before David took over Carlisle, it raises the questions: where were the walls before David? Or were there just gates and no walls? Or was it just that David raised the height of the existing walls?

David strengthened the Castle and City because he obviously saw trouble ahead once the in-fighting between the English Royal family was sorted out and was getting ready to mount a stout defence of his territory.

Alas for David, in 1153 he died, and the throne of Scotland was taken by 11-year old Malcolm IV. The following year, 1154, the Royal in-fighting in England ended and Henry II became King of England and demanded Carlisle back from the Scots. Malcolm, now 12, obviously decided that even with its strong defences, it would be difficult to defend

Carlisle against Henry II's forces, and handed it over.

The next major burst of building at the Castle came during the reign of Edward I. Edward I came to the English throne in 1272. By 1284, after a long and bloody campaign, he had conquered Wales and added it to his territories. In 1290 he turned his attention to conquering Scotland. Carlisle, as the city on the border between the two countries, became a major player in his plans, and the base for his planned invasion.

Under Edward I, Carlisle Castle became more than just a military garrison, it became the seat of Royal Government, a place where the Royal court gathered. A Great Hall was built to host royal occasions. The Keep was enlarged to accommodate prisoners. The Castle became the store house for the planned invasion: not just for food and ammunition, but for the large siege weapons that Edward was planning to use against the Scots. The stage was set for Carlisle Castle to play a major role, not just in the history of the immediate area, but in the whole troubled history of the relations between England and Scotland.

A favourite spot for tourists, sitting on the wall in front of the Cathedral's magnificent East Window.

36

6 - THE CATHEDRAL

Along with the Castle, the most notable Norman building still standing today in Carlisle is the Cathedral.

As we have seen, the Romans were very adept at hi-jacking local traditions and incorporating them into Roman rule to make the conquered locals feel part of the picture. The early Christian Church was equally adept at incorporating pagan events and structures into its own religion to help convert the locals: incorporating festivals from the religious calendar of other religions into their own calendar (e.g. in the Julian calendar 25 December was the date of the Winter Solstice and was regarded as The Nativity of the Sun, because from that date the days begin to lengthen. The Romans celebrated the birth of their own God, Mithras, on 25 December. The early Christians added this date into their own calendar and claimed it for their own). The early Christians also built churches on sites of pagan worship, obliterating the original paganism in the process.

As we saw in the Introduction, Carlisle was named after the pagan God, Lug (Caer-Lug aka Caer-Lluel). The knowledge of where the

Above:The Cathedral in the eighteenth century..

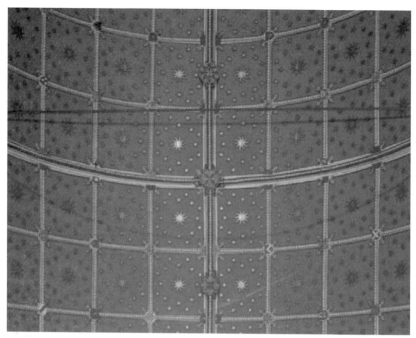

The interior of Carlisle Cathedral, with the magnificent ceiling designed by Owen Jones, showing a host of stars.

specific place of worship of Lug was in the area of Carlisle seems to have long since vanished. Today it could even be buried beneath the site of a Burger Bar, the new religion where gi-normous portions of fries (which bear more similarity to fried wallpaper paste than they do to potatoes) are worshipped. However, it is possible that the first Christian church in Carlisle was built near the site of a pagan Viking graveyard, if the results of an archaeological dig near the present Cathedral are correct.

In the early 680s King Ecfrith gave the Christian missionary St Cuthbert an area of land in Carlisle close to the remains of the old Roman town for him to build a church and a monastery. As well as St Cuthbert's church another place of Christian worship, St Alban's chapel, was built in Scotch Street.

In 1122 King Henry I came to Carlisle and decided the city's places of worship needed to be in the Norman style to go with the Castle he was having built. So the old pre-Norman buildings were knocked down and their stone recycled into a new Norman style church and a new priory known as St Mary's. In 1133 these came under the command of Aethelwulf, first Bishop of Carlisle, and thus the church became The Cathedral.

As you will find elsewhere in this book, the Cathedral and Priory suffered a turbulent history, along with the rest of Carlisle. In 1292 it was partly destroyed by fire, and a hundred years later the work to repair the damage had still not been completed.

In 1385 an argument at the Cathedral became so heated and bitter that it led to a riot in which the priests were dragged by an angry mob out of the church into the streets. The argument had its roots in the election of the post of Prior in 1381. The election had been between two men: William de Dalston and Thomas de Warth. Dalston was the cellarer of the Priory, the man in charge of the wine. Warth had been the cellarer immediately before Dalston took the post. The dirty tricks of the election campaign, particularly by those who favoured Dalston, would do credit to the spin doctors of modern politics.

According to a statement made to the bishop by one of Dalston's supporters, Thomas de Warth had been "stupid, incompetent and negligent" during his time as cellarer. He had brought the Priory to near bankruptcy. This statement went on to say that Thomas de Warth had been excommunicated some seven years before as a result of him violently assaulting another Canon, one Richard de Everwyk. And, even worse, this same Thomas de Warth had carried on an adulterous affair with the wife of Walter Gunter of Carlisle.

Faced with a smear campaign worthy of any modern tabloid newspaper, it may come as no surprise that Dalston won the election. Whether the success went to Dalston's head, it is not known. What is known is that, once elected Prior, Dalston began to make life very difficult for his Bishop, Bishop Appleby, refusing to accept many of the Bishop's decisions. Rumour has it that the row between Dalston and the Bishop was fuelled by Dalston's former electoral rival, Warth, and his supporters. Finally, on 12 August 1385, Bishop Appleby had had enough, and he excommunicated Dalston, with orders to the parish priests of St Mary's and St Cuthbert's to publish the Notice of Excommunication in their

A misericord from under a Cathedral seat showing a very angry wife scolding a very chastened husband.

churches. Unfortunately for the poor parish priests, as soon as they tried to do so, Dalston's supporters invaded the churches and tried to snatch the Bishop's Notices of Excommunication from them. The priests hung grimly on to the Notices, and as a result they were hauled out into the street by the angry mob, still clinging determinedly to the Notices.

With things escalating out of control, the King, Richard II, and the Archbishop of York were forced to intervene. By now Dalston's opponents were accusing Dalston of carrying on an adulterous affair, and in September 1385 Dalston resigned as Prior, but remained as a Canon.

However, Dalston was not a person to take things lying down and Go Quietly. In 1390 there are reports of Dalston and Richard Everwyk (the same Richard Everwyk who Warth had been accused of violently assaulting in 1381) "gathered some soldiers of the town and forcibly resisted the bishop and prior". Once again the Archbishop and the King were brought into the situation, and Dalston and Everwyk reluctantly promised to behave in future.

In 1541 the Priory was stripped off its assets by Henry VIII as part of his policy of Dissolution of the Monasteries.

In 1745 and 1746 captured Jacobite soldiers were held prisoner in the nave of St Mary's, and spent most of their time doing as much damage to the place as they could.

In 1797 the author, Sir Walter Scott was married at the Cathedral.

One of the most noticeable features of the interior of the Cathedral is the ceiling. It was decorated by Owen Jones in 1856 to feature a whole host of stars. Unfortunately most visitors to the Cathedral miss the ceiling because it is so high and very few people can be bothered to raise their heads and look directly upwards. This could be because experience has shown them that when they do they invariably: a) trip over something; b) get bumped into; c) get mugged; d) afterwards they suffer from a very stiff neck. The superb ceiling in Carlisle Cathedral is worth risking all of these for.

7 - 14th CENTURY: FIRE, SWORD AND THE PLAGUE

It is not generally known that there were originally actually Five Horsemen of the Apocalypse: War, Famine, Plague, Vengeance and Fred. However Fred spent most of his time drifting around on his horse thinking lovely thoughts, writing poetry, and smelling flowers. As a result he was cast out of the League of the Horsemen of the Apocalypse as Unsuitable Material, leaving just the Famous Four Deadly Ones to roam the earth bringing misery to all they encountered. And in the Fourteenth Century, these Four descended on Carlisle with a vengeance, and stayed around the area for most of the century:

As we have seen, the tone of "Destruction by Fire" had been set just before the Fourteenth Century in 1251, when most of Carlisle was destroyed by fire; and again in 1292 when Simon of Orton burnt down most of the city while setting fire to his family's house in a fit of pique.

The Fourteenth Century started in much the same vein: in 1303 a serious fire destroyed Rickergate and part of Botchergate.

Above: The muniment chest from the Guildhall Museum. It was made in 1400 and was meant to be fireproof. It was also extra secure since it had four locks which could only be opened when four city officers met together.

As far as "Destruction by the Sword" goes, the blame for much of what happened during the Fourteenth Century could be said to rest with **Edward I.**

In 1290, King Edward I of England decided to go on the offensive and bring Scotland under his control. He had already carried out the same sort of campaign in Wales (1276-1284) which had brought Wales into his kingdom. Scotland was his next target.

However, before he could begin his efforts at conquest by fire and sword, events played into his hands. In 1286, King Alexander III of Scotland had died, and onto the throne stepped, or rather toddled, his 3-year old grand-daughter, Margaret, daughter of King Erik II of Norway, as all Alexander's children had predeceased him. At the time she ascended to the Scottish throne, Margaret was living in Norway.

Aware that having a 3-year old Queen on the throne put them in a difficult, not say to rather weak, position against a tough King like Edward I, the Scottish lords approached Edward with the idea of uniting their two countries by marriage: what did he think of the idea of Scotland's young Queen Margaret marrying Edward I's son, Prince Edward of Caernarvon, aged 2?

Edward thought it was a pretty good idea: to add Scotland to his kingdom without having to fight for it, so in 1290, having thought about it at some length, Edward I accepted on behalf of his son, and plans were laid for the marriage of Margaret (by then 7 years old) to Prince Edward (by then 6 years old).

A boat was sent to Norway to bring Margaret to Scotland, but on the journey young Margaret fell ill and died. The wedding was off.

With Margaret's death, the rivalries between the different Scottish families for the throne came to a head, and it looked as if Civil War would break out. There were plenty of candidates who all laid claim to the throne, though some of them had claims that were a bit weak (eg: they were the illegitimate son of someone who once had ridden a horse owned by a cousin of someone who had once lent a much earlier Scottish King some money and never been paid back.) In the end it came down to two major rivals: John Balliol and Robert the Bruce.

The Bishop of St Andrews, desperate to avoid major bloodshed, approached Edward I on behalf of the Scottish lords and asked him to arbitrate and choose one of these as the new Scottish King.

Feeling rather miffed that he'd missed out on getting hold of Scotland so easily ("If only Margaret had survived the boat journey! I've always said long sea journeys can be dangerous!" etc. etc.), Edward chose John Balliol as the one he thought he'd be able to control better, and so he would still be able to get control of Scotland without a fight.

Edward was right. In 1292 John Balliol became King of Scotland, and immediately pledged homage to Edward.

If only Edward had left it at that things would have been fine. Unfortunately for Edward, and for Carlisle, he began to throw his weight about in Scotland, and let John and the Scottish nobles be aware in no uncertain terms that they were all subordinate to him as King of England. That he, Edward I, was Top Dog, and they'd better not forget it. And, by the way, I think a few more taxes would be in order.

After a while, John began to resent being treated like this, and in 1296 he rebelled against Edward. The Anglo-Scottish Wars had begun.

One of the first acts of rebellion by John's forces was an attack on Carlisle by the Earl of Buchan and his army. This assault was notable for the resistance to the onslaught by the women of Carlisle. At the time Buchan's men attacked the city there were no soldiers in Carlisle to defend it, only the townsfolk. A Scottish spy who was being held inside the city walls managed to get free and started a fire, which soon spread through the city. The men of the city left their defensive positions on the wall in a panic as they rushed to and fro in a) an attempt to put out the fires; and b) catch the spy before he could do any more damage. Seeing the city walls undefended, the Scots took this opportunity to launch their attack on the city walls and gates, putting their siege ladders up against the walls. However, just when the Scots thought they were home free, the women of Carlisle took over the defences on the city walls and began to pelt the climbing Scots with stones, and also poured boiling water down on them.

The Scots were forced to withdraw. First victory in the Anglo-Scottish Wars to the women of Carlisle.

Robert the Bruce saw this state of chaos as a chance to win Scotland for himself, and he sided with Edward I, and took on the defence of Carlisle Castle.

In July 1296, after a series of battles, with Robert the Bruce fighting alongside Edward I's army, King John was forced to surrender, and Edward took over the Kingdom of Scotland.

Robert the Bruce began to drop strong hints that Edward had him, Robert, to thank for defeating John, and wouldn't it be a good idea if he, Robert, looked after the Scottish Throne for a bit; just to keep it warm.

Edward's answer was quite firm: No. He was King of Scotland, as well as England and Wales, and anyone who thought differently would have to fight him for it.

This was not a wise move. As the Romans had discovered to their cost some hundreds of years before, the Scots were a formidable enemy.

From now, the north of England, and particularly the Carlisle area, became Edward I's home base as he carried on his war against the Scots, while the Scots laid siege to Carlisle with great frequency, and Edward counter-attacked with such ferocity he earned himself the nickname "The Hammer of the Scots".

In 1297 Scottish resistance against Edward and the English increased, led by William Wallace (of "Braveheart" fame). Wallace launched an attack against Carlisle, but this time the city was better defended, with 14 crossbowmen and 95 foot-soldiers in the city under the command of Henry de Percy. Wallace had no equipment for mounting a proper siege, and in the face of Henry de Percy's professional troops, and also mindful of what the Earl of Buchan had told him about Carlisle's Warrior Women, Wallace withdrew. Wallace was captured by Edward's forces in 1305 and executed.

In 1306 Edward I arrived at Lanercost Priory before heading for Carlisle, which was to be his northern seat of Government, but his ill-health forced him to stay at Lanercost until March 1307. In November 1306 Edward I had sent out a message to all the knights and would-be knights across his kingdom, summoning them to a Parliament at Carlisle in January 1307. This meant that Carlisle became overcrowded with huge numbers of would-be warriors and would-be dignitaries, in addition to the vast retinue that goes with Government.

In December 1306 Edward, the Prince of Wales, arrived at Carlisle with his army to join his father in his War against the Scots. Because Edward I was very ill, certainly too sick to launch his attack, the Prince and his army stayed in Carlisle and waited for the King to recover. While they waited they did what armies have often done in the past: ran riot and caused mayhem in the town. Prince Edward and a few of his friends kept the "arson" tradition alive by burning Wetheral Priory. To the locals it must have seemed a choice between a rock and a hard place: to be invaded by enemy Scots who burnt the town and caused havoc, or by so-called "friendly English" who did the same.

By July Edward claimed he had recovered sufficiently for his major offensive against the Scots, and he led his army to Burgh-by-Sands, to the west of Carlisle, ready to launch an attack across the Solway Firth, and there, on the marshes, he died. A monument marks the spot on the marsh where he died, within sight of Scotland.

If Edward I was "The Hammer of the Scots", his son, Edward, was The Limp Handshake and a King who was Not To Be Trusted.

Following a series of raids by the Scots on Carlisle, most of them led by Robert the Bruce (in 1311, 1315 and 1316), Edward II decided to try another tactic. In 1322 he appointed Sir Andrew de Harcla to be Earl of Carlisle. He asked Sir Andrew to conduct secret negotiations with Robert the Bruce to see if some sort of deal could be sorted out - (e.g. that Robert the Bruce only laid siege to Carlisle on Thursdays and Sundays when there was an "R" in the month, and didn't actually kill anyone.) The thing was, Edward stressed, was that these negotiations must be Really Secret with a capital S. Edward's father had been known as a strong man, and Edward II didn't want to be thought of as a wuss by comparison.

However, the problem with Secret Negotiations is that more than one person knows about them, which meant that sooner or later someone reported back to Edward that Sir Andrew de Harcla was involved in some kind of secret talks with Robert the Bruce.

Edward II, who, as we said, was a King Who Could Not Be Trusted, said he was shocked at such treason, and summoned Sir Andrew to York.

Sir Andrew, having his doubts about the King and being suspicious about what lay in store for him if he went to York (a quick trial and a complete denial by the King that Sir Andrew had been acting under his orders, followed by execution) refused to go. So Edward sent the Sheriff of Cumberland, Sir Anthony de Lacey, to arrest Sir Andrew for high treason.

Realising that Sir Andrew was very well guarded inside Carlisle Castle, Sir Anthony sent a message to Carlisle asking Sir Andrew would he mind if Sir Anthony called in at Carlisle Castle for a private chat and a drink or two, purely social, just himself and a couple of close friends.

Believing that Sir Anthony, as a fellow Cumbrian, could be trusted, Sir Andrew replied, "Not at all, drop in whenever you feel like it." Which Sir Anthony duly did, his close friends being three armed knights. They arrested Sir Andrew before he could raise the alarm, and then the small army which Sir Anthony had brought with him from Cockermouth, who were waiting in a horse lay-by along the road, took command of the castle.

That was the end for Sir Andrew. After being found guilty of High Treason, his sword was broken over his head and he was stripped of his clothes of official office. He was then hanged, drawn and quartered. His head was put on a spike on London Bridge. The four different quarters were put on show at Carlisle, Newcastle, York and Shrewsbury.

As for Edward II, he met his end in 1327 in a most painful way: a red hot poker was pushed up his rectum. To prevent any Sherlock Holmes of the day discovering the crime, the assassins first thrust the pointed end of a hollowed out cow horn into Edward's anus and then pushed the poker through that into his intestines, so that the red hot poker would leave no external marks.

After Edward II died in 1327, he was succeeded by his son, Edward III. In 1328, by the Treaty of Northampton, Edward III abandoned English claims on Scotland.

However, the Scots had not abandoned their claim to Carlisle and the surrounding area.

In 1345 a series of attacks by the Scots laid waste to much of the area outside the city walls. Fire and sword continued, with houses being set alight constantly.

On one occasion, a citizen of Carlisle called Allen Gunson was so shocked to find that his house was on fire that he threw everything he owned out into the street in an effort to save it. The result was that his neighbours ran off with his belongings and he never saw any of it again.

This climate of riot and disorder even infected religious events of the day. On Sunday 31 July 1345 a Miracle Play was being performed in the market square in Carlisle. An argument broke out between two men. One of them was a servant of the Bishop of Carlisle, Bishop Kirkby, the other was a servant of a local businessman, Peter de Tilliol. The argument became so intense that the mayor and the local bailiffs became involved.

De Tilliol sent for the Bishop to try and end the row, but the Bishop's response was to send 30 armed men to defend his servant. The Bishop's soldiers arrived and let off a volley of arrows, killing a poor innocent bystander who'd just come over to find out what all the row was about.

This led to a full-scale running battle between the Bishop's soldiers and the townsfolk, which only stopped when word spread that the Scots were about to attack Carlisle again.

In 1349 the third member of the Quartet of the Apocalypse, Plague, came in the form of The Black Death, killing, it is guessed, as much as two third of the population. Those who survived this first brush with Plague didn't escape for long, because The Black Death returned to Carlisle in 1361, 1369, 1379 and 1391.

As if this was not enough, King Edward III imposed a Poll Tax on the city in 1377, which caused many of those who had survived fire, sword, siege and plague to finally pack up and leave the city rather than pay the tax.

Those who stayed in Carlisle may have thought they'd got over the worst, but Fate had another dice to throw. On 4 May 1391 another devastating fire destroyed almost three quarters of the city. Rickergate, Botchergate, Castle Street and St Cuthbert's Church all vanished in the flames, as did nearly two thousand houses.

It could be this whole series of continuing disasters during the Fourteenth Century that helped develop the famous Cumbrian attitude of stoicism, of putting up with all the miseries that Malign Fate throws at you "without twining" (without moaning about it).

8 - THE WARS OF THE ROSES

If the people of Carlisle thought that things could only get better with the arrival of the Fifteenth Century ... they were wrong.

In 1399 Henry Bolingbroke (now known as Henry IV) had claimed the Kingship of England after forcing Richard II from the throne. Disputes over Henry's claim to the throne led to a time of uprising and rebellion from within England. At the same time the Scots were set on getting the north of England back into Scotland. In all of these, Carlisle figured greatly.

In 1402 Henry IV told his council that a large force of Scots "had been in our kingdom near our vill of Carlisle in number around 12,000 and done what evil they could, but praised be our Lord this was little." "Little" perhaps in the King's opinion. For the residents of Carlisle, to be attacked by a force of 12,000 Scots was no minor event but a Major Disaster which resulted in Death, Damage and Destruction.

Above: An artist's impression of the vast priory which dominated the medieval city.

49

In 1403 the Percie family of Northumberland, who had many interests and supporters in the Carlisle area, rebelled against Henry IV and joined forces with the Scots against the King. Over a period of five years, until the Percie family was finally defeated in 1408, skirmishes and raids between the Percie family and their supporters in Cumberland, and Henry's troops, brought devastation to many areas around Carlisle.

By 1409 a report on Carlisle said, "the Gates and a greater part of the Walls have Fallen to the Ground".

At this point the French entered the game, throwing their hand in with the Scots in an effort to get rid of Henry.

In 1424 a truce was declared between the English and the Scots, much to the relief of the people of Carlisle. At last, they thought, better times are finally here. Once again ... they were wrong.

In the 1430s Carlisle was struck by plague. Bad weather led to terrible flooding, which destroyed the harvests. Cattle died as a result of disease and starvation. Not that Carlisle was alone in suffering this way at this time, but it was the length of time that Carlisle had to endure one disaster after another which made it worse for the folk of the city. In 1436 a very hard winter struck the area. There was a failure of the harvest in 1437. In the summer of 1438 excessively heavy rain destroyed the grain crop, resulting in another failed harvest. Also in 1438, 1439 and 1440 cases of plague were reported in Carlisle and the surrounding areas. The result of this was starvation and death.In the 1430s Carlisle was struck by plague. Bad weather led to terrible flooding, which destroyed the harvests. Cattle died as a result of disease and starvation.

In the 1440s and 1450s there were more attacks by the Scots, which finally led to a full scale war between England and Scotland in 1456. All this at the same time that England was being torn apart by the War of the Roses - the Red Rose of the House of Lancaster against the White Rose of the House of York.

The Wars of the Roses was one of those very confusing family quarrels, with one side blaming the other for everything that has gone wrong since the invention of the wheel and refusing to talk to each other at family weddings, christenings and funerals. Epic books have been written about it and Shakespeare wrote plays on the subject. From the point of this book, we are only interested in how it affected Carlisle.

The main contenders in this War were Edward IV of York and Margaret of Anjou, wife of King Henry VI (the Lancaster half of the feud). In 1461 Queen Margaret of Anjou promised the Scots they could have Carlisle if they helped her capture it for the Lancastrian side. Unfortunately, when Margaret made her offer, she did not specify that she wanted Carlisle left standing and in habitable condition. The Scots attacked Carlisle with the same vigour they had used on previous occasions. They destroyed Upperby and the area known as Caldcotes, the Tithe Barn, and while they were at it they also destroyed the city's gates and mills. This was the sort of thing they had attempted to do many times before. It was only after they had finished destroying the city they remembered that Margaret of Anjou had given Carlisle to them to keep. So, feeling rather foolish, the Scots stood around in the ruins of Carlisle for a bit, shuffling their feet in an awkward and embarrassed manner, before one of them said, "Well, I never liked the place anyway", and then headed back over the border to Scotland.

To the great relief of the people of Carlisle, after hundreds of years of death, destruction, misery and high taxation, things now quietened down. The Wars of the Roses ended, and for the next few years, the Kings carried on their soap-opera of intrigue, murder, betrayal and refusing to get on with the rest of the family, but they did it at a safe distance: in London and the south of England.

In 1483 it looked as if the Wars of the Roses might break out again during the reign of Richard III, and people in Carlisle hastily started boarding up their windows and checking their insurance policies, but fortunately for northern Cumbria, the fighting was kept around Bosworth Field, where Henry VII gained victory, and the throne of England.

Life returned to a kind of peace, where people could worry about other things than attacks by Scots, attacks by claimants to the throne, plague and such things, and get on with worrying about the real issues of life: e.g. why is it that when you finish washing clothes there is always an odd sock left over; why, when you drop bread, does it always fall on the buttered side?

Trade in the city flourished, especially with the Scots. This may seem unusual as for so many years the Scots seemed to have spent most of their energies attacking Carlisle, but it has to be borne in mind that there is a big difference between politics (leaders of nations who decide who they will and won't declare war on) and ordinary Joe Public and Hamish McPublic who just want to get on with their lives and earn a reasonable living. Carlisle was helped by the fact that after 1482 there were only two places in northern England where Scots could legally conduct trade: Carlisle and Berwick.

One enterprising Scot called Gilbert del Chambre (a good old Scottish-sounding name) arrived in Carlisle with some pairs of boots for sale. Such was the success of this venture that a few weeks later he returned to Carlisle with 40 cattle, which he sold. With the money he bought a load of boots. A year later there are reports of this same Gilbert del Chambre exporting cloth and leather from Carlisle in large numbers, and thinking of calling himself "Del Chambre Cows and Boots International Limited."

Scotland was not the only market for the traders of Carlisle: A salesman called Thomas Denton bought a load of sheepskins in Carlisle and took them to Newcastle to sell. However, the people of Newcastle turned their noses up at these sheepskins and Thomas found himself with more sheepskins on his hands than he had anticipated. Rather than do what many 21st Century traders would have done, which is put up a sign that said, "Sale Sale Sale - Massive Price Reductions! Sheep Skins at give away price - Buy One Get One Free!" or similar, Thomas loaded his sheepskins on to a ship bound for Holland and sold them there. With the proceeds he bought a load of iron in Holland, which he brought back to Carlisle, and sold at a profit. Sheepskins and iron . . . from such beginnings are Retail Empires built!

Gradually Carlisle became known as a major trading centre, with people coming from far and wide to buy and sell. Sales of leather and cloth flourished, bringing employment to the people of Carlisle who got work as tanners, weavers, glove-makers. Every worker had money to spend and needed food to eat, so bakers, butchers and brewers also grew rich.

In this atmosphere of peace and prosperity, the monks and friars of the Priories in Carlisle now returned to doing Good Works, Praying and living a life of Quietness and Repose. At last, they thought, they could return to a quiet and a secure life far away from threats of war and a life of constant harassment. They were wrong.

9 - THE TUDORS

In 1536 King Henry VIII (he of Six Wives fame) was counting the money in the Royal Counting House and reflecting that there wasn't a lot of it. It wasn't just the wives that had taken their toll of the royal purse, Henry had also engaged in wars against both the French and the Scots, and - as many a King before him had found out - Wars are an expensive business. In the 21st Century the answer for Henry would have been easy: he would have simply telephoned one of those Loan Companies who advertise on day-time television offering to consolidate all your debts providing you hand over your house, your children, your dog, and most of your internal organs. Henry VIII had no such choice.

It was then that his advisers mentioned to him that the monasteries and priories dotted around the country seemed to have an awful lot of money. Certainly far too much for people who were supposed to live a life of simplicity, eating only dry bread and drinking water and meant to spend

Above: The Elizabethan Guildhall as it appeared in the eighteenth century. Today it is a museum and an Italian restaurant.

A The Castle.
Botchergate

The North

Caldew gate

The Citie off

Carlesle
Viardgate

The Citie off

B

C
D

The grene frosch on bant

The East

A The Castle.
B Cathedral Church of St. Mary.
C Church of St. Cuthbert.
D The Market Place.
E The Citadel.

CARLISLE
in the reign of
QUEEN ELIZABETH

Scale of Feet.
50 100 200 300 400 500 600

54

most of their time praying and giving out charity. In fact, the King's advisers pointed out to him, there didn't seem to be much charity being given by these religious folks to the King. And for people who were supposed to live lives of simple poverty, there seemed to be an awful lot of gold and jewels in these monasteries. And good food. For example, they pointed out, at the Priory in Carlisle the canons (the Top Dogs at the Priory) had lots of servants, including a butler, a brewer, a carpenter, a laundress, someone to clean the toilets, a tiler, a candlemaker, and a cook, who even had an assistant cook to help.

When they checked the menus at the Priory they found the meals included fish, white and red herrings, salmon, oxen, sheep, piglets and geese. And instead of it being served plain and dry and bland and tasting of nothing but sawdust, as one would expect of such religious folk, the food was seasoned with mustard, raisins, sugar, ginger, caraway, almonds and pepper. What was more, at meals these so-called pious monks drank red wine and ate biscuits afterwards! And they didn't leave a tip for the waiter!

"In short, your Majesty," the King's advisers murmured to him, "these Religious Places are a Very Profitable Business just ripe for being Nationalised with all the money going to the State. In this case... You."

And so it was that in 1536 Henry VIII announced his policy of Dissolution of the Monasteries, in which all the rich monasteries were closed down and all their wealth went to him. It was a prime example of a Take-Over followed by Asset-Stripping.

Fortunately for Carlisle, it was a long way from London, and for a while the Canons and Priors at Carlisle must have thought they would be missed out, but as everyone knows, Tax Collectors get you in the end. On 9 January 1541 the King's Commissioners arrived in Carlisle and began to close the Priory and strip it of its assets. Suddenly the monks, priors, friars and canons of Carlisle found themselves holding a medieval version of a P45 in their hand, plus a penny for redundancy, and kicked out into the street, along with their butler, brewer, carpenter, laundress, toilet cleaner, tiler, candlemaker, cook and assistant cook.

The local townspeople took the opportunity of the visit by the King's Commissioners to point out that there were large gaping holes left in the city walls from all the attacks by the Scots over the years, including

Henry VIII had a major impact on Carlisle. He dissolved St Mary's Priory in Carlisle as part of his policy of "Dissolution of the Monasteries". He employed a Bavarian engineer, Stefan von Herschenperg, to rebuild the Castle and build The Courts (the Citadel).

some bits where the walls and gates had gone completely, and possibly with all the money the King was getting from selling the goods and chattels from the Priory in the market, it would be nice if he found his way to put some of the money into repairing the city walls, just in case the Scots decided to attack Carlisle again.

Grudgingly, but aware that as he was still at war with both Scotland and France, and as Scotland wasn't very far away from Carlisle as the crow flies, Henry ordered the City and Castle walls rebuilt. To carry out the work he appointed one Stefan von Haschenperg from Bohemia, believing in the new adage Vorsprung Durch Technik (loosely translated as "German engineering is best".)

One of the two towers built at the south entrance to Carlisle by Henry VIII's Bavarian engineer. Rebuilt over the centuries by other engineers, including Thomas Telford, it still stands today while some of the buildings constructed in Carlisle during the 1960s and 1970s have had to be demolished.

Von Haschenperg set to his task with great energy: he strengthened the inner wall of the Castle, made sure there was sufficient space to put cannons in place along the walls, and added the famous half-moon battery that can be seen today.

Von Haschenperg went even further: he erected massive defences outside the castle to protect it, creating another castle outside the original castle.

Spreading himself even further around the town, and determined to create the most impregnable Castle ever built, Von Haschenperg moved his army of workers to Botchergate and set them to work to build two large drum towers with a massive new gate between them. Such was the quality of this incredible piece of German engineering that within fifty years much of the building work had fallen down and had to be rebuilt.

However, at their completion the two large drum towers, known as the Citadel and the Courts were highly impressive, as was the new and improved Carlisle Castle, which was strong and tough, defiant against all who would lay siege to it. There was just one problem. This new Castle was built to have formidable firepower as its main defence. But by 1545, the guns to defend it still hadn't been delivered. It was rather like having a car built, and then being unable to drive it because you were still waiting for the wheels to arrive. The problem lay with the King, who was not prepared to fork out good money for guns when he felt that a few peasants armed with a pitchfork or two sheltering behind these new improved battlements would do.

Von Haschenperg protested to the King that without the guns his artistic vision was incomplete, and demanded that the King put cannons in place.

This was not the way to talk to a man who was used to getting his own way with wives, Popes and mothers-in-law, and so Von Haschenperg found himself sacked and on his way back to Bohemia, muttering darkly to himself about the dubious character of British royalty, and wondering if he fitted an engine to the wheels of a cannon and called it the Volkswagen Beetle anyone would be interested in it.

10- THE BORDER REIVERS

Henry VIII died in 1547 and was succeeded in rapid succession by his 9-year old son, Edward (who died 6 years later); then by his daughter Mary (aka Bloody Mary) who reigned for just five years, and finally in 1558 by his youngest daughter, Elizabeth; also known as Good Queen Bess and The Virgin Queen.

It was during Elizabeth's reign that Carlisle Castle became the prison for two famous prisoners: Mary Queen of Scots, and William Armstrong of Kinmont, also known as Kinmont Willie,a notorious Border

Above: The Border Reivers were English and Scottish families in the Border region who lived by robbery, plunder, murder and pillage for hundreds of years. Any Law Officer sent to quell them was either killed or bribed. They were finally defeated by James I who crushed them with a policy of "fire, sword and summary execution". The picture shows Kinmont Willie escaping from Carlisle Castle.

A serious moment contemplating the Cursing Stone. The Stone is inscribed with the excommunication curse pronounced by the Bishop of Glasgow in the sixteenth century.. Recently it made national headlines when a local councillor blamed the stone for all the city's problems.

Reiver, though the conditions in which both were kept were vastly different.

In May 1568 Queen Mary landed on the coast of Cumbria with her "posse" of twenty women and a load of servants. She claimed to be an asylum seeker, seeking refuge from people in Scotland who wished her harm. Elizabeth, however, had her doubts: there were those who said that Mary was going to try and claim the throne of England and Scotland for the Catholics from Protestant Elizabeth. And so Elizabeth said that Mary was very welcome indeed, and suggested that she stay as her guest at Carlisle Castle for a short while.

Mary's time at the Carlisle was hardly the traditional view of prison life: living on gruel and water and, after a hard day's labour breaking rocks, being flogged. On the contrary, the life which Mary spent while at the Castle is one for which most people would willingly commit crimes: servants, pleasant walks around the Castle, a fire in her rooms, as much food as she could eat, and all of the best quality. And no rent to pay.

Far different was the incarceration of Kinmont Willie: he was brought to Carlisle in chains in 1596. But then, Kinmont Willie was a Border Reiver.

As we have seen, the Border between England and Scotland had been a bone of contention between the two countries, with each laying claim to Carlisle and the surrounding areas. At various times Carlisle had been part of Scotland, then part of England, then part of Scotland, then part of England again . . . and so on.

In the same way that there were questions over which country ruled this area, there were also questions over who policed it. As a result, the Border area was often seen as a place without law, a place where anarchy ruled and the more powerful and the more cunning stole from the weak.

In 1249 an attempt was made to try and bring some sort of Law and Order to the Border area. The Border was split up into three regions known as Marches: East, West and Middle Marches. Each of these Marches was to be under the control of a March Warden. These Wardens were appointed in 1297. Carlisle was part of the English West March. It was separated from the Scottish West March (which consisted of the areas of Kirkudbright and Annandale) by a large area known as The Debateable Land. This area was twelve miles long and four miles wide, and the people who lived in this area did not come under the control of either English or Scottish Laws. The result was that families whose occupation was robbing and looting moved into this area of land and carried on their careers from the Debateable Lands, untroubled by The Law, unless they encountered the Warden while they were out plundering in the March areas.

These families were known collectively as The Border Reivers, and included such well-known families as the Armstrongs, the Bells, the Grahams, the Nixons and the Littles, among others.

Obviously this situation did not go down well with local non-Reivers, who were regularly robbed, raped, killed and ransacked by the Reivers, who would then rush back to their bases in the Debateable Lands before the forces of Law and Order could catch them. Appeals to the Kings of both England and Scotland were made for these bandits to be controlled. The problem was that many of the families in the Border area were related to one another, by marriage or conquest, and the Kings realised it was doubtful whether any locally appointed March Warden would actually arrest members of his own extended family. So the March Wardens in the English Marches generally came from the far south of England, appointed by the King to keep order.

The theory may have been good but in practice it was awful and of no help to local law-abiding citizens at all. There were two main reasons for this: 1) The Border was a long long way from any authority and back-up forces in the South of England. 2) The wages paid to the Wardens was a pittance, certainly not enough for any man to risk his life for. And so the Wardens supplemented their income by taking bribes from the Reiver families to turn a blind eye to all the robbing, rape and pillage. Either that, or the Wardens mounted what they termed "official raids against wrong-doers", in which they took a party of thugs across the Border and took back what they believed the Reivers had stolen, plus a bit extra. These "recovered articles" never found their way back to the people who had lost them to the Reivers, the Warden kept them, or sold them. The Wardens also took prisoners and ransomed them back to their families.

In short, the Border area was a lawless place where the Lawkeepers, the March Wardens, were often as crooked as the Reivers themselves.

Of course, being a March Warden may have been a profitable job when carried out along these lines, but the Reivers understandably objected to their loot being stolen from them, and so they, in turn, set about killing the Wardens. In 1537 a March Warden called Roger Fenwick was murdered at Bellingham by "three naughty persons". In 1585 Lord Russell, another Warden, was shot and killed.

To try to give some appearance that the system of Law and Order in the Borders worked, and that guilty robbers could be apprehended and compensation paid to their victims, Truce Days were set up. Truce Days lasted from sunrise to sunset, and at agreed points along the Border on Truce Days people could gather and make a complaint about being robbed. If the robber had been caught, then that robber would appear at that point on Truce Day, usually in chains, and pay compensation to their victim before being released. The theory was that on Truce Days, rival families and warring factions would meet and try and sort out their differences without bloodshed, under the watchful eye of the March Warden. The number of people each warring family was allowed to send was limited to no more than a thousand (showing how large these families were), but in reality, as arithmetic and counting wasn't very high on the educational curriculum of those days, the numbers who turned up were vast.

To add to the party atmosphere that was supposed to be happening on these Truce Days, market stalls were set up, strong drink was sold, and the crowds would be entertained by jugglers and musicians. In other words, it was like an early version of Glastonbury.

Although these Truce Days were supposed to be peaceful affairs, as you can imagine, put a few thousand bitter enemies in the same overcrowded place, ply them with strong drink, and expose them to a few Medieval Singers and Mime Artists to really annoy them, and Truce Days often turned into violent open warfare, with dead bodies being dragged off in all directions.

One interesting aspect of the Border Reivers was that they were non-Nationalistic. Scottish Reiver families would happily kill and rob Scots as well as English, and vice-versa. And on many occasions, if there was a lot of wealth to be gained, then Scottish and English Reivers would work together to carry out a raid. Of course, the English March Wardens blamed the Scottish Reivers for all the mayhem that went on, and the

Scottish Wardens likewise blamed the English Reivers. If they had laid the blame on the Reivers on their side of the border, then the Wardens would be expected to Do Something About It.

So, for hundreds of years, the people of Carlisle and the surrounding areas not only had to worry about being attacked by official Scottish armies and official English armies whenever a war broke out, which seemed to happen with alarming regularity, but also being robbed and plundered by Scottish and English robber families, the Reivers.

By the time of Queen Elizabeth I, most Wardens had given up any hope of bringing the bandits under any sort of control. The Reivers murdered and plundered as they liked. Things had got so bad that the Warden of the time of the Western March, Lord Scrope, even suggested rebuilding Hadrian's Wall, complete with mile castles, to stop the Reivers coming over the Border; but when Elizabeth (who was notoriously tight with a penny) learnt that to rebuild the Wall would cost £30,000, the idea was kicked into touch.

Much miffed, Lord Scrope was determined to stop the Reivers doing just as they liked whenever they liked. One particularly notorious Reiver was William Armstrong, also known as Kinmont Willie. In 1596, while Willie Armstrong was returning from the festivities of a Truce Day with a load of other Reivers, he was set upon by soldiers under the command of Thomas Scrope, son of Lord Scrope, arrested, and thrown into the dungeons at Carlisle Castle.

The other Reivers were outraged, claiming that this was Very Unfair Indeed, that Willie had been arrested during a Truce Day. Lord Scrope replied that it was sundown when he arrested Willie, so the Truce Day was officially at an end. And as far as Lord Scrope was concerned, he had captured a notorious and dangerous Reiver and he was now locked up safely in Carlisle Castle, and that was where he was going to stay, until he could be tried, found guilty, and executed. It looked like a triumph for the Law and Order Party.

Unfortunately for Lord Scrope, the Castle was not in as good a state as it should have been in view of all the repair work that had been carried out by Stefan von Hershenperg. Despite von Herschenperg's claims that Bohemian engineering was the best in the world and would last for a couple of millennium, some of the walls he put up only fifty years before had already started to fall down, and there were gaping holes in others.

A party of Border Reivers, led by Lord Buccleuch (also known as Sir Walter Scott), carried out a night-time raid on the Castle and rescued Kinmont Willie. Because of the guerrilla-style tactics of the raiders, plus the large holes in the Castle Walls, the soldiers on duty didn't even notice the rescue was going on until Buccleuch and his men, along with Kinmont Willie, were actually leaving the Castle.

In 1603 Queen Elizabeth I died childless (being a Virgin Queen was not very helpful in producing an heir), and James VI of Scotland became James I of England, uniting the two countries. At that time there was a tradition that the rule of Law and Order was temporarily suspended between the death of one monarch and the announcement of the succeeding heir (or heiress) to the throne. Possibly it was hoped that in such circumstances everyone would treat the death of the monarch with respect and not do anything wrong. However, this was not the case with the Reivers - they were a Bad Lot and Proud Of It. They took advantage of the time gap between the death of Elizabeth and the proclamation of James to cram in as many robberies, murders and general mayhem as they could. In one raid alone a combined force of Grahams, Elliots and Armstrongs raced into Cumbria and stole 5,000 cattle and sheep. King James saw this as the Reivers cocking a deliberate snook at his authority as the new King, so one of his first announcements was his intention to put an end to the rule of the Reivers. Many other rulers had tried this before, but James pulled no punches in his proclamation, which read: "The late Marches and borders of the two realms of England and Scotland are now the heart of the country. Proclamation is to be made against all rebels and disorderly persons that no supply be given them, their wives or their bairnes, and that they be prosecuted with fire and sword."

The Reivers must have chuckled smugly at this, with an attitude of "Yeh, so what? We've heard it all before! Typical politician, trying to impress the public by making speeches and promises when he knows there's no way he can keep them. Words are easy, let's see what happens when he tries to take action!"

What happened was pretty dramatic: James abolished the Border Marches. From now on, said James, there was no such place as The Border, the area would be known as the Middle Shires. He also set up a

Commission of five Englishmen and five Scotsmen with orders to bring the area formerly known as "The Border" under control. This Commission was based in Carlisle, and they were given unlimited powers. An example was a new Border Law which James passed, which said, "If any Englishman steal in Scotland or any Scotsman steal in England any goods or cattle amounting to 12 pence he shall be punished by death." For good measure the Law added that these executions did not need a trial. Almost immediately 140 of the most notorious Reivers were rounded up and hanged without trial. This policy of arrest and execution without the bother of a trial was known as "Jeddart Justice". The surviving Reivers realised that King James meant business, and some of them decided it was better to be on the winning side. One of these was Lord Buccleuch, who immediately became an ally of the King and helped his new Royal Best Friend by capturing and hanging as many of his former criminal colleagues as he could lay hands on.

The Reiver families who suffered most were the Grahams, the Elliots, the Armstrongs and the Nixons, many of whom were given a choice of death or exile. Wisely, many of them chose exile, and many of them headed across to the New World that Sir Francis Drake had claimed for Elizabeth some years earlier.

Once there, their descendents set about making themselves prominent in this new land. We can see how successful some of them were following the celebrations to mark the first landing on the moon in 1969. At that celebration there were three men on a podium together: the astronaut Neil Armstrong, the American President, Richard Nixon, and the country's spiritual adviser, Reverend Billy Graham . . . Armstrong, Nixon and Graham, good Reiver names all.

11: 1644 - 1645: SIEGE!

The English Civil War (Cromwell's New Model Army, also known as "The Roundheads", vs King Charles II's Cavaliers) began in 1642.

Many Scots had sided with Cromwell, possibly in the belief that anyone who wanted to get rid of an English King was alright by them. In 1643 a contingent of Scots under the command of David Leslie laid siege to Carlisle, which was a city loyal to King Charles. However, as sieges went, this one was pretty short-lived when Leslie gave up and withdrew with his men to Newcastle. There were rumours at the time that the reason Leslie withdrew his forces was because Carlisle was on the point of surrendering, and as Leslie and his men would only be paid by Parliament up to the time that Carlisle fell, withdrawing made sure that Leslie's army

Abovr: Tullie House, the home of the Tullie family. Isaac Tullie was the author of a book about the siege of Carlisle in 1644-1645, based on his personal experience of the siege during the English Civil War.

Carlisle Cross stands in front of the Old Town Hall in what was the market square. This particular cross was put up in 1682, although there had been a cross on the same place much earlier. It is from the steps of this Cross that important announcements are still made which affect the city and the country.

kept being paid for a lot longer than if they'd had a quick victory.

In 1644 a combined armed force of Cromwell's men and Scottish forces defeated the Royalists at Marston Moor, and effectively the whole of northern England came under the control of Cromwell and Parliament. The exception was Carlisle, which had a garrison under the command of Sir Thomas Glenham that still remained loyal to the King. General Leslie was ordered to lay siege to Carlisle once again, and this time not to leave until he'd finished the job. Leslie's army of Scots and Roundheads arrived at the walls of Carlisle in October 1644.

Considering that Leslie's army was 4,000 strong, and Sir Thomas Glenham only had 700 soldiers in the city, the expectation was that the Parliamentarians would launch a fierce attack and overwhelm Carlisle by sheer force of numbers. However, Leslie appeared to have a different strategy in mind: stay outside the city and glare at the enemy within, while taking things easy. In fact what few attacks there were seemed to be carried out by the soldiers inside the city, who would rush out of the gates every now and then to steal provisions and cattle from the soldiers laying siege. When that happened the soldiers of Leslie's army would rush after them and try and get their cattle and provisions back.

On the humanitarian side this method of conducting warfare had a lot to commend it: unlike previous states of siege where hundreds of soldiers and civilians died in a bloody and terrible fashion, this method led to no-one dying at all, except from old age and other natural causes, although some cows and chickens were severely frightened.

By Christmas 1644, conditions inside the city walls of Carlisle were getting grim. Food was running low. Most of the domestic animals inside the city had already been eaten, and people were starting to eye one another not as friends and neighbours, but as walking joints of meat.

By April 1645, many of the horses had been turned into food, and the few horses that were left standing found their feed trough pretty empty. By June 1645 even horse was starting to be thought of as a luxury, and people were reduced to eating dogs and rats. Many of the soldiers who were supposed to be defending the city examined their current diet of roasted rat and hempseed and found it wanting, and began to sneak out of the city and started surrendering.

Sir Thomas Glenham, however, refused to surrender the city to the

View of Carlisle across the River Eden from Stanwix Bank.

Roundheads. He insisted he would stick it out until the bitter end. The Bitter End came on 24 June 1645, when Charles I's forces were defeated at Naseby. On 25 June, Glenham surrendered Carlisle.

The Scottish forces remained in Carlisle until 1647, when they left and the English Parliamentary forces arrived to occupy it.

In 1648 there was an uprising by Royalist forces, determined to retake Carlisle and have the King returned to the throne, and once more Carlisle became a Royalist stronghold. However, this didn't last long. In October 1648 Cromwell himself arrived at Carlisle, and the city surrendered once again to the Parliamentarians.

Whether Cromwell was fed up with Carlisle changing sides every time there was an uprising or an attack on it, or whether he was just fed up with having a King around as a reminder of The Good Old Days, the result was that in 1649 Charles I was executed. This put a rather abrupt end to the Royalist cause (at least for a few years), but it in its place came Inter-Religious Rivalry.

Up to the time of Henry VIII there had been markedly little Inter-Religious Factionalism, as there had basically been only one religion in England and Scotland: the Catholic Church. The Jews had been persecuted by the Catholic Church, but that persecution had been going on for so long that it had become just "one of those things".

Since the time that Henry had brought in The Church of England as a rival to the Catholic Church, there had been a whole new raft of religions springing up all over Britain, and the Borders area found itself in the middle of them.

The Calvinist John Knox had already been storming around the area in the 1560s with his Protestant message of fire and brimstone for all Catholics and anyone who dared to favour the trappings of a life of luxury, such as soft clothing and cushions to sit on.

In 1653 the Quaker, George Fox, preached the Quaker message in what remained of Carlisle Cathedral.

The overall fashion of the times was penance, gloominess, harsh clothes, hard beds to lie on and hard chairs to sit on, and the Fear of Damnation if you enjoyed yourself too much; a way of life much favoured by the puritan Oliver Cromwell. Then in 1658, Cromwell died. He was succeeded as Protector by his son, Richard, but enough people muttered darkly that, "He's not the man his father was", and so Richard was kicked out in 1660 and replaced by King Charles II, son of the beheaded Charles I. Royalty was back in charge of the country again. Once more the country was ruled by a Monarch, and once more Carlisle became a Royalist city.

12. THE JACOBITE REBELLIONS

After Charles II died his brother, James, became King James II. James II upset a great many people by wanting the Catholic faith to be dominant. As a result in 1688 James was sacked as King by the politicians and James's Protestant daughter Mary, and her Dutch husband, Prince William II of Orange, were offered the throne of England.

James II, however, wasn't giving up so easily. He put together an army of Scottish and Irish Catholic soldiers, and rumour had it that he was going to march with them on Carlisle. Why Carlisle is not exactly clear. Possibly it was because Carlisle had been the object of attack by so many armies over the centuries that it had become a matter of habit. The first thing a leader did was say to his second-in-command: "Right, we are now ready to revolt/crush the rebellion! (Depending which side they were on.)

Above: Scotch Gate. The heads of some of the Jacobite rebels of 1745 were hung over this gate as a grisly reminder to other would-be rebels that attacking Carlisle would not go unpunished.

72

Where shall we attack first?" And his second-in-command would say "Well, Carlisle looks a good bet. Everybody always attacks Carlisle. The people there are used to it. They might even be disappointed if we don't attack them first." And so Carlisle would be laid to siege.

In this case, the mere rumour of an attack by James's Catholic forces was enough to cause panic. However, before James could actually launch his attack against Carlisle, Sir Christopher Musgrave arrived in the city on behalf of William and Mary and Parliament and demanded that the city of Carlisle hand itself over to Parliament and the new Dutch monarchs. Carlisle was quick to do so, and the city's defences were reinforced.

Concerned that his attack on a reinforced Carlisle might fail, and if that failed then the rest of his campaign would suffer, James II decided to delay his offensive in pursuit of the Crown, and instead he went to France with his family to write his memoirs and try and gain greater support for a rebellion. He never returned from France.

In 1707 the Act of Union was passed, which brought the Parliaments of England and Scotland together. "Hurrah!" cried the people of Carlisle, "Now we are one country at last, the Scots will stop attacking us!"

As so many times before, the people of Carlisle were wrong.

When William and Mary took over England (and Scotland, Ireland and Wales) James II's son and legitimate heir to the throne, James Edward, was dropped from the list of Potential Kings or Queens. This obviously rankled with James Edward, and after his father died in 1701, he got to looking across the English Channel as the years passed and thinking to himself, "I was supposed to be King there!"

The trouble for James Edward was that he didn't just leave it at thinking about it and talking about it to friends and fellow exiles as they supped jars of ale in French bars and munched croissants. When George took over the throne in 1714, James Edward was so put out that he had been overlooked again as King that he decided to Take Action and Do Something About It.

George I was a German who spoke no English. There were those who thought this was a bit much: first a Dutchman gets the job of King of England; then a German. It was a bit like the argument over who was going to be Manager of the English Football team: why were the homegrown choices for the job being overlooked? As far as James Edward was concerned, he was the homegrown choice and ought to be on the throne of England (and Scotland, Wales and Ireland) as James III.

In October 1715 James Edward launched an uprising in Scotland to make himself King, with a force of 1,200 foot soldiers and 600 horse soldiers, which, as all Scottish Uprisings Against the English seemed to do, headed in the direction of Carlisle.

Surprisingly, for once, this invading Scottish army missed Carlisle by a few miles and ended up at Brampton, about ten miles to the east of the city. Whether this was because they held the map the wrong way round as they crossed the border, or whether the Scots were just fed up with attacking the same old city ("Not Carlisle again! Can't we attack somewhere different this time?"), it is not known. The people of Brampton were certainly surprised to find themselves being marched on by an army of Scottish invaders, and after being told by them that they were invading in the name of James III, must have asked them, "Are you sure you're not looking for Carlisle?"

The Irish Gate, to the west of the City, was also known as Caldew Gate.

English Gate and the Old Gaol. In 1803 William and Dorothy Wordsworth visited the forger, John Hatfield, who was in the Gaol under sentence of death to give him moral comfort and read him some poems. It is said that Hatfield was heard to groan: "Not daffodils again! Just hang me and get it over with!"

The invaders did not stay long in Brampton, just one day, possibly reflecting that there was even less to do in Brampton than there was in Carlisle. At least in Carlisle there was a Castle to destroy. The Scottish Invaders headed for Penrith, where they met a force of 14,000 militia that had been assembled by Lord Lonsdale and the Bishop of Carlisle to defend England. 14,000 English militia against 1,800 Scots must have looked pretty good odds on paper, but the quality of the men who made up this Militia had obviously not been examined too closely before they were recruited. As the Scots advanced on Penrith, the 14,000 English militiamen took one look at them as they advanced with kilts swirling in the breeze, claymores clashing and pipes wailing, and fled in confusion. At the sight of their huge army running away, Lord Lonsdale rushed off to hide in Appleby Castle and the Bishop of Carlisle locked himself up in his bishopric seat at Rose Castle.

This must have cheered James Edward up enormously, and he and his army set off on the next leg of their journey towards London, determined that this time next week he would be on the throne as James III. Unfortunately for James Edward their next stop was Preston, and here they came up against a much more determined opposition, and were forced to surrender. And that was the end of the Jacobite rebellion ... or, at least it was as far as the new German King, George, was concerned.

However, James Edward's son, Charles Edward Stuart (also known as Bonnie Prince Charlie, aka "The Young Pretender" to differentiate him from his father, "The Old Pretender") had obviously spent so many years listening to his father muttering, "That throne of England ought to belong to us by right of birth", that thirty years later he decided to have a go at putting himself on the throne. In August 1745, Bonnie Prince Charlie landed in the Western Highlands and raised an army of 5,000 Catholic Scottish sympathisers, and then headed towards England. As usual, Carlisle, being just across the border, was their first point of call.

In fact Bonnie Prince Charlie's attack on Carlisle got off to a rather inauspicious start. His army arrived at Carlisle on Saturday 9 November. Charlie should have checked this out first, because Saturday was shopping day for the people of Carlisle and the surrounding area, and when the army of Highlanders arrived outside the walls of Carlisle, they couldn't get in because the roads were filled with shoppers heading home after having bought their weekly provisions at Carlisle market. All they could do was stand around outside the city walls and look threatening, while being jostled by shoppers.

This also caused a problem for the soldiers inside the city who were supposed to be defending Carlisle against the invasion. The defending soldiers had expected that the Scots would choose any day to arrive but shopping day. Because the Scots had chosen to arrive on a Saturday and had got mixed up with the people taking their shopping home, they couldn't fire on Charlie's Highland army for fear of hitting a shopper or two.

By the time the shoppers had all gone home it was getting too late to start a battle, so the Scots asked if they could be put up for the night inside Carlisle, as it was November and very cold and they only had their

The Old Town Hall. Between the Town Hall and the Cross was the city bullring, where bulls were baited. Bull baiting was brought to an end in Carlisle in 1792, despite protest from some locals that it was a "traditional sport" and to ban it would affect their way of life.

kilts to keep their private parts warm. The defending soldiers refused their request, and so Charlie's men were forced to spend the night outside.

The next day the leader of Bonnie Prince Charlie's army demanded the garrison surrender and hand Carlisle over to him. The answer was a cannon fired at his troops from the walls of the Castle, which they took to be a "No". (In fact it was unlucky for Charlie that advance word about his invasion had reached Carlisle a month or two earlier, because when the soldiers inside the Castle heard about Bonnie Prince Charlie and his advancing army, they thought it might be a good idea to inspect the few cannon they had, and they were horrified to discover that that the touch-holes of their cannons (where the fuse was lit) had been plugged up with wooden pegs by some naughty small boys.)

So, as had been the case so often before, a siege was set in motion, with the Scots outside the walls of Carlisle demanding the soldiers inside surrender, and the soldiers inside, under the command of Lieutenant Colonel James Durand, refusing.

However, it is likely that the defenders had heard too many tales of the last time there had been a siege of Carlisle by Scots forces, one hundred years earlier, with the people caught inside the city being forced to eat horses, dogs, rats, straw, and generally having a hard time, because on November 15 1745, Lt Colonel Durand surrendered, and the triumphant Highland Forces entered Carlisle. Bonnie Prince Charlie himself arrived in Carlisle two days later. He obviously wanted to wait until the battle was over before putting himself in the front line.

Charlie appointed a governor for Carlisle, as well as a new bishop, one Thomas Cappock. Leaving a garrison of Highlanders behind to keep Carlisle under his control, he set off south to continue his advance on London, as his father had done 30 years before. In this venture Charlie went further than his father: James Edward had only got as far as Preston before being defeated. Bonnie Prince Charlie made it to Derby before his army were beaten. The remains of his defeated army headed north to Scotland in disarray. Charlie must have reflected that his hopes of gaining the English throne may have been lost, but he still had one ace left: the city of Carlisle. On 19 December Charlie left a garrison of 400 of his men in Carlisle to keep control of the city for the Jacobite cause while the rest of his army fled north over the border. On 21 December, the Duke of Cumberland and his army, in hot pursuit of Bonnie Prince Charlie's retreating army, arrived outside Carlisle and laid siege to the castle and the city. By the end of December 1745 it was all over: faced with cannons and a huge and disciplined army the Jacobite Rebels surrendered, on the condition that they "would not be put to the sword". Cumberland kept to his word: instead of putting them to the sword, he hanged many of them instead.

Even after the hangings, Cumberland still had a large number of prisoners on his hands and nowhere to put them, so the Duke imprisoned them in Carlisle Cathedral, where the Highlanders proceeded to make their feelings known by drawing graffiti on the walls, as well as using the place as a toilet, and generally vandalising the place. On 10 January 1746 the prisoners were taken from the Cathedral and sent to proper secure accommodation at Lancaster and Chester, leaving the Cathedral clergy with a major clean-up to do. Official complaints were lodged by the Cathedral authorities about the state the cathedral had been left in by the prisoners: "The Rebels made a most nasty church. Cleaning and washing proves of little use for the flags (the flagstones on the floor of the Cathedral) being old, spongy, and ill laid, the earth under them is corrupt and till that is removed the Cathedral church will not be sweet, not will it be safe to have service in it."

On 16 April Bonnie Prince Charlie and his army of Scottish rebels were finally defeated at Culloden. Carlisle was one of the places where 370 of the rebel prisoners were sent to be tried. Some were condemned to be hanged, but the majority were sent to North America as "transported prisoners".

After the end of the Jacobite Uprising, Lt. Col. Durand was court martialled over his surrender of Carlisle in November 1745, at which he produced the written statement he made at the time of the surrender: "The Militia of the Countys of Cumberland and Westmorland, and also the Militia of the town of Carlisle, having absolutely to a man refused to defend the castle, and the Garrison consisting only of two companions of invalids amounting to 80 men, many of whom are extremely infirm, and the castle very large, so that there are neither men to manage the guns nor man the walls, and the Mayor and the inhabitants of the town together with the officers of the militia having sent to treat with the Rebels against the opinion and protest of Colonel Durand, Captain Gilpin, and the rest of the officers of the Garrison, and being refused any terms, and threatening to destroy both town and militia with fire and sword unless the castle be surrendered, it is our opinion that the castle being not tenable, it is for his Majesty's service that it be abandoned, as it will be absolutely necessary for the preservation of the lives of his Majesty's subjects, who would otherwise be exposed to inevitable ruin." In short: the men wouldn't fight, the Mayor was already making a treaty with the enemy, and there were only him and Captain Gilpin and a few very old and very infirm invalids to defend this place against 5,000 Highlanders. Lt. Col. Durand was found not guilty.

The rest of the Eighteenth Century passed without too much in the way of Major Events. The Scots didn't attempt any further invasions and Carlisle remained remarkably siege-free. Possibly the most notorious

MARGERY JACKSON is Carlisle's most famous miser. She was born in 1722. When her father died in 1732 she shared the inheritance of his wealth along with her mother and her two brothers. However, by 1752 her brothers had died, both without children, and her mother had also died, and Margery inherited the lot, and was determined to hang on to it. It was rumoured that she kept all her gold and jewels in an iron chest in her house, and it was said that she kept a loaded pistol ready in case anyone tried to break into her house and burgle her chest.

It is often quoted that money does not bring happiness (usually said by the rich; the poor also say that lack of money does not bring happiness, either . . . but no-one listens to them.) In Margery's case, despite all her money she was a

miserable person who spent her latter years glaring fiercely at people as she walked the street of Carlisle dressed in rags. When she died in 1812 aged 90 her estate was valued at £50,000, worth millions in today's terms, and she became the richest woman in the graveyard.

thing to happen in Carlisle towards the end of the Eighteenth Century was the "Mushroom" election of Sir James Lowther. In 1786 there was a General Election, and Sir James Lowther, Earl of Londsdale, was standing as a candidate. However, Sir James had stood before, and each time had been defeated, so this time he took positive steps to make sure he got elected. Only Freemen of the City were allowed to vote, so Sir James made 1,400 of his employees from the West Cumberland Coalfields Freemen of the City of Carlisle, on the understanding that they would vote for him. This sudden large number of Freemen of the City appearing overnight out of absolutely nowhere became known as "mushrooming", and the election was called "The Mushroom Election" by Sir James's political opponents, and most of the press of the day. Not surprisingly, Sir James was elected. Also, not surprisingly, his opponents made an objection and the election result was overturned by a Parliamentary Select Committee.

The Station today. Court Square remains a very attractive, though busy, part of the city.

13 - THE RAILWAY

Before the Railway came the Canal. But before the canal came the dream of Carlisle being the major port in the north of England, the gateway to the rest of the Known World (and the Unknown World, until it could be discovered.) There was one problem with this: Carlisle was inland from any stretch of sea with any depth worth talking about. The nearest stretch of open water was the Solway Firth, but at low tide even this might only hold a couple of feet of water, barely enough to float a plastic duck, let alone a ship big enough to sail to America and Africa. And so, in the Nineteenth Century, a canal was built linking Carlisle and the tiny coastal village of Fisher's Cross some twelve miles west of Carlisle on the Solway Firth. Fisher's Cross was renamed Port Carlisle, causing

Above: Carlisle Citadel Railway station opened in 1847 and still looks much the same today as it did then..

83

The Port Carlisle Dandy. A serious case of overcrowding in the railway carriage.

some problems for the postmen of the time who had never heard of any such place, but gradually they got used to it, and Port Carlisle is the name it still bears today.

The intention was for large ocean-going ships to moor at Maryport, and cargoes to be taken to and from these large ships along the Solway Firth from Maryport to Port Carlisle by smaller boats, which would then navigate the canal to the Carlisle basin. After decades of planning, the canal opened on 12 March 1823.

In 1824, with goods now able to travel from Carlisle to all parts of the world, an even more ambitious proposal was made: that the canal be extended right across England to Newcastle, which would link the Irish Sea and the North Sea. Effectively Britain would be cut in two with a canalway going right across it from sea to sea.

Estimates of the cost of the canal were put together. At the same time estimates were drawn up for constructing a railway along the same route. The canal came in at £888,000; the railway at £252,000. Hardly

The canal basin in 1820, when Carlisle had serious ambitions to be a port.

surprisingly, the canal proposal was dropped. The railways won.

The Newcastle and Carlisle railway opened for business on Saturday 4 November 1837. The cost of the single journey was 9s 6d (47.5p) if you wanted to sit in the comfort of a closed carriage and look out at the view through a window, or 7s 6d (37.5p) if you didn't mind braving the weather in an open carriage. The weather in November in Cumbria and Northumbria is not noted for being warm and sunny, so no doubt the closed carriage seats (First Class) sold out pretty quickly, with only The Very Poor and masochists sitting in the open carriage.

The idea of travelling by train at what were then colossal speeds spread like wildfire across north Cumbria. Soon everyone was jumping on the Railway Bandwagon. Everyone wanted a piece of railway in their area.

In 1837 the Maryport and Carlisle Railway Company was authorised, which came into effect in 1845. However, this caused problems for the Port Carlisle canal company. The port at Maryport was larger than the one at Port Carlisle; and the rail journey time to Maryport was much faster than taking a small boat from Carlisle along the canal.

Customers who wanted to get to and from Carlisle and the coast quickly preferred to go to Maryport by rail, rather than dawdle along the canal via Port Carlisle. Soon the canal company was facing financial ruin. In desperation the directors of the company decided that if they couldn't beat 'em, they'd join 'em. In 1854 the canal between Port Carlisle and Carlisle was filled in and a railway track was laid along the route.

Unfortunately for the Port Carlisle Canal (and now Railway) Company, every other place in north Cumbria was getting in on the act and rail tracks were appearing all over the place. In 1856 a railway line between the Solway coastal town of Silloth and Carlisle opened. This line connected with the Port Carlisle to Carlisle line at Drumburgh, a village a few miles to the east of Port Carlisle. Soon Silloth was a thriving seaside resort as townies from Carlisle flocked to this Eden on the Sea to laze on the beach, swim in the sea, and spend time lounging around in one of the new hotels and guest houses that had sprung up. Before long the majority of rail traffic along this route was going directly between Carlisle and Silloth, train loads of happy holiday makers and goods, while the branch line between Drumburgh Junction and Port Carlisle had fewer and fewer customers using it.

In 1857 the inevitable happened: the steam train was taken off this branch line and replaced by a carriage pulled by a horse along the railway tracks, known as The Port Carlisle Dandy. The Dandy carried on operating until 1914, when the line between Port Carlisle and Drumburgh was closed for good.

Meanwhile, in Carlisle, rail travel was the new wonder way to get about, and there was a proliferation of stations in the city. The railway line from Maryport to Carlisle ended at a station in Crown Street. The line from Newcastle arrived at a station on London Road. The terminus for the line from Silloth was at the canal basin. But the Big Railway Line, the one with the major connections to the two large cities of London and Glasgow, had recently been completed, and their railway station was a join venture between the LNWR (London North Western Railways) and the Caledonian Railway Company, a brand new station known as The Citadel, which was begun in 1847 and finished in 1848. The Citadel Railway Station was a magnificent structure and the other railway companies must have looked at it in envy. Gradually these other railway companies managed to worm their way inside The Citadel, and soon The Citadel was their terminus as well.

By 1870 there were 138 passenger trains using the Citadel Station every day.

In 1876 the final piece in the railway jigsaw was completed when the Settle to Carlisle Railway line opened, adding even more trains to those passing through The Citadel. At last, after hundreds of years of waiting since the Steam Engine had first been invented, train spotters in North Cumbria finally had something to look at.

14 - THE 19th CENTURY: INDUSTRIAL CARLISLE

After centuries of battles, wars, plague and Reivers, Carlisle faced a new problem in the Nineteenth Century: industrialisation. Industrialisation itself wasn't the problem, it was the situations it caused.

In the old days the textile industry was based on home workers using spinning wheels and weaving looms to produce cloth. Various inventions towards the end of the Eighteenth Century revolutionised this process: particularly the spinning jenny patented by Hargreaves, Arkwright's water frame, and Kay's flying shuttle. During the early years of the Nineteenth Century the power loom was introduced, resulting in a weaving machine that could work even faster and produce even more

Above: Dixon's Mill seen from the old water mill in Dentonholme. Previously weavers had been Free Range in their own homes, but were now packed into large buildings. After this experiment was shown to increase productivity among humans, it was repeated with chickens.

cloth. But not every home could accommodate a power loom .. in fact most homes at that time were thought luxurious if they had two rooms and an outside toilet. So the textile workers moved out of their rural cottages and away from their small simple craft-machines and headed for Carlisle to work on larger machines in large factories.

Weavers from rural Cumbria weren't the only ones attracted to the factories: with rumours that the streets of Carlisle were paved with gold, families from Ireland and Scotland flooded into the city, driven from their own countries by poverty and desperate for work of any sort. The problem was that with so many people desperate for work, wages were forced down to the lowest possible level. The poor at the bottom of the heap stayed poor, but worked long hours to earn their money.

In 1801 there were 5,745 people living in the central area of Carlisle, and 3,882 living in the outer areas (Botchergate, Rickergate and Caldewgate), a total of 9,627. By 1831, these numbers had increased to 8,356 in the inner city, plus 10,713 in the outer areas, a total of 19,069. A massive increase in the size of the population without a similar increase in housing or facilities.

The result: Carlisle became a city with too large and too poor a population for its size, with inadequate sanitation, and with poverty and malnutrition rife. In short, huge areas of Carlisle became slums. A Report of the Carlisle Sanitary Association in 1850 reported: "In Rickergate ward the Committee can hardly find words to express the amount of filth. Cholera has claimed numerous victims in East Tower Street and Drover's Lane. In Moffat's Yard there is only one privy for 28 families. Other properties are without proper conveniences at all. In some of the lodging houses more than 20 people are living in one room, and that adjacent to the filthiest privies and dunghills."

For the mill-owners, however, business boomed. The tall imposing marvel at Shaddongate that still towers 300 feet over Carlisle to this day is Dixon's chimney, built at Shaddon Mill in 1836 by Peter and John Dixon, sons of the founder of the firm, Peter Dixon Snr. Shaddon Mill was a huge employer of people, its machines powered by steam from seven huge coal-fired boilers.

Much of the cloth produced in these mills came from cotton. Raw cotton came from the United States. In 1861 the Civil War broke out between the North (the Union) and the South (the Confederacy) over the issue of slavery, and the supply of raw cotton from America stopped. This was a major blow for Carlisle's textile industry. When the American Civil War ended in 1865 and slavery was abolished, the final blow fell for Carlisle's cotton mills. Previously all the large plantations in the American south had bought huge supplies of gingham to make clothes for its negro slaves, and nearly always in the same pattern. Now the negroes were no longer slaves, they did not want to wear a cloth that reminded them of their enforced bondage. Sales of gingham collapsed.

In 1872 Peter and John Dixon and their partner, Joseph Forster, were declared bankrupt.

In 1888 Shaddongate Mill was converted to woollen spinning by Robert Todd and Sons, and in 1919 Linton Tweeds was set up on the site. The tradition of woollens and knitwear still survives today in the shadow of Dixon's Chimney, mainly through smaller firms.

Textiles weren't the only major industry in Carlisle during this time, there were also Biscuits, namely Carr's Steam Biscuit Factory (now McVitie's).

John Dodgson Carr was a Quaker, like many other business men in Carlisle during the Nineteenth Century. (A word of explanation may be needed here, as some readers will be saying, "Who or what were Quakers?" The Quakers, or to give them their proper name, The Society of Friends, are a religious organisation founded in the middle of the Seventeenth Century by George Fox. Fox believed God could be worshipped without the pomp and ceremony found in most churches. In fact he didn't believe that churches were really necessary at all, believing that God could be worshipped anywhere. Although this sounds a pretty reasonable and moderate view in modern times, in the Seventeenth Century Fox was seen as some sort of Religious Terrorist, and spent six years in jail. At one of his trials Fox told that judge that he should "tremble at the word of God", and the Judge snapped back that Fox and his followers were nothing more than a bunch of "tremblers or quakers", and that's how the religion got its name. The basis of Quakerism is concern and consideration for all humans, which is why Quakers are also pacifists and at times of war refuse to fight but instead work in ambulance services and the like. The Quaker businessmen of the Eighteenth and Nineteenth

Rudd Women on the steps of Carlisle Cross in 1895. They were called Rudd Women because they collected a soft red stone called "rudd" from the bed of the river Caldew and sold it. This red stone was used by local householders to give a red finish to their window sills and doorsteps.

Centuries saw "work" as not just something to be endured for five days a week in order to get enough money to go out and get roaring drunk on Saturday, and then pray for forgiveness on Sunday, but believed work should be something that improved people's life in all ways: morally, as well as financially. Now, with the explanation over, back to the story . . .)

John Dodgson Carr, a baker, came to Carlisle in 1831 and shortly after set up Carr's Steam Biscuit factory in Caldewgate. Being a Quaker, he wanted his workers to have Good and Improving Conditions to work in, as well as biscuits, so he provided small but sanitary houses for his employees; and in addition he installed hot baths, a reading room and a library all near his factory. By 1846 his well-read and clean workers at the factory were producing 400 tons of biscuits every year.

Another businessman from the same Carlisle Quaker congregation as John Dodgson Carr was Hudson Scott. He started with a printing and stationery business, but in 1876 he developed a method of printing transfers on tin plate, and so he started producing decorated tin packages for the biscuits made by his fellow Quaker, John Carr. Together they created the perfect present for Christmas: biscuits in a tin with a pretty picture on it.

Yet another Quaker who set up in business in Carlisle was James Laing, a builder. James Laing came to Carlisle from Sebergham and set to work constructing houses. As the population of Carlisle expanded, so James Laing's construction business grew.

Hat-making was another industry for which Carlisle was famous. In fact, Carlisle had been well-known for hats since the mid-Eighteenth Century when William Nelson had set up his hat-making business, followed by R G Ferguson early in the Nineteenth Century. The largest hat manufacturers in Nineteenth Century Carlisle were William Carrick & Sons, who continued making hats into the Twentieth Century, until the firm was taken over by Kangol in the 1950s.

One major effect of the rise of all these industries in Nineteenth Century Carlisle was to turn Carlisle into a city known for its prowess in engineering. Blacksmiths had always been a vital part of the scene in North Cumbria. Now their trade expanded as they took on the needs of the new heavy industries springing up all over the city.

Foundries were set up, making accessories and parts for the large machines that drove the textile and food industries. These large machines needed men to maintain and repair them. The new railways needed parts and skilled engineers. New engineering works appeared around Carlisle. Some of these engineering works went on to become major players, others went broke, and some were bought by large companies eager to expand and take advantage of this New Industrial Age (as was the case with George Richardson's St Nicholas Engineering Works on London Road, which went bankrupt and was bought by Cowan Sheldon and Co).

By the second half of the Nineteenth Century, the massive rise of industrialisation, along with the expansion of the railways, had combined to turn Carlisle into one of the most important manufacturing cities in the whole of Northern England.

However, despite the prosperity this expansion brought to many in the city, and despite the benevolent aims of employers such as Laing, Carr and Scott, the majority of the population of Nineteenth Century Carlisle lived in appalling conditions. Among the worst of the slums were in the area known as The Lanes in central Carlisle. It was estimated that between nine and ten thousand people lived in the alleys and lanes between Fisher Street and Lowther Street, though it was hard to establish the actual figure as people were crammed into tiny hovels and slept in rotas. It may have kept the beds permanently warm in winter, but it also kept the beds well populated with fleas and every disease that the various occupants could carry. The only momentary refuge from the awful grind of daily life was Drink. And fortunately for the citizens of Carlisle, Drink was readily available.

Brewing in Carlisle on a large scale had started in the mid-Eighteenth Century when Richard Hodgson and James Atkinson set up The Old Brewery on the north side of Caldewgate in 1756. In 1774, Pattrickson & Co set up the New Brewery on the south side of Caldewgate, at Shaddongate. In 1790 West Walls Brewery was set up and in 1794 the High Brewery was started. The High Brewery was bought by Joseph Iredale in 1832 and twenty years later it was being described as "one of the most complete breweries in the North of England". With 11 fermentation vats, the brewery was able to produce 250 barrels of beer a week.

Iredale's High Brewery moved to Currock Mill in 1875 as a result of the expansion of the Citadel Railway Station.

In the Nineteenth Century three other breweries were set up in Carlisle: the Meadow Brewery, the Queen's Brewery, and the Crown Brewery.

As any Sociologist of the Temperance persuasion will tell you at the drop of a hat, and will then continue to lecture you as you are trying to leave the room to get away from them, this proliferation of breweries pouring beer into the pubs and off-licences of Carlisle, combined with an expanding population living in poverty in slum conditions breeds crime. Theft and robbery in Carlisle reached epidemic proportions.

Not that this drink-driven crime wave of the late Nineteenth

Jimmy Dyer, Carlisle's famous street entertainer and fiddler. A statue of Jimmy Dyer can be seen outside Debenhams in the Lanes Shopping Complex.

Century was a new phenomenon. Carlisle had been considered a lawless place for a long time. Early in the Nineteenth Century, proposals had been made to set up a proper police force in Carlisle to try and clamp down on lawlessness and crime, but the members of the local Corporation refused. They insisted that the two Constables who were in charge of keeping Law and Order throughout the whole of Carlisle could manage perfectly well. It was pointed out to the Corporation that it might be thought of as a bit of an exaggeration to even call two police officers "a Police Force", and that until the police car was invented, or at least the police bicycle, it was impossible for these two lonely plods to police such a large area as Carlisle and the surrounding district on foot. The Corporation dismissed these criticisms and said that if things got out of hand they could call on the soldiers garrisoned in the Castle. (The soldiers were there to protect the city against any further attacks or invasions by the Scots over the border, as well as to deal with threats of invasion by the French and the Irish. Despite there having been no further invasions from Scotland since the Jacobite rebellion of 1745, after 800 years of attacks from Scotland, the good Burghers of Carlisle were taking no chances, whatever the politicians in London might say

The Hiring Fair which took place in the Market Square in Carlisle. Here we see a girl being hired out in 1904 for a contract fee of 1/- (5p).

about there being no further threat from Scotland.)

A cynic might say that the reason the politicians who were in charge of Carlisle didn't want to increase their force of constables from two lonely beat bobbies was because they didn't want to pay out any more money. After all, the Upper Class in Carlisle who were in charge of things were fairly safe from being the object of crime. They lived in the richer areas, while the criminals tended to operate in the poorer or middle-class areas.

Things changed in 1826. In that year there was an election and the Tory candidate, Sir Philip Musgrave, decided to go to Caldewgate to give a rallying speech to the weavers in that area, urging them to vote for him. Musgrave was assured of a large crowd because a) there wasn't much else to do in Carlisle in those days, and b) Musgrave had brought along a load of his cronies and most of the Corporation to support him, and many of the weavers were curious to see what The Upper Class looked like at close quarters.

To Musgrave, it may have seemed a good idea at the time, a politician getting to know The People, but The People weren't very impressed. Some of the crowd heckled and others shouted out questions. Unfortunately for Sir Philip, his answers did not meet the approval of the gathering. It is always irritating for starving poverty-stricken people to be told by some well-fed politician that their well-being is going to be in safe hands if they vote for him. The crowd grew unhappy, then restless, and finally a riot broke out, and during it the crowd grabbed Sir Philip and put him on a weaver's loom. The rest of Sir Philip's entourage were thrown in the mill pond.

As the riot seemed to be getting worse a magistrate was called for. He swore in 30 men as Special Constables to deal with the situation. However, the Mayor of Carlisle discovered with some concern that every one of these new Special Constables was a weaver, and was more likely to join in ducking Sir Philip and his companions in the mill pond rather than arresting any rioters, so he refused to use them. Instead, the Mayor went to the scene of the riot, accompanied by the two regular constables. There, the Mayor read the crowd the Riot Act and told everyone they were all under arrest. This was either the act of a Very Brave Man or of a Very Stupid One. In the popular fiction of the time, the crowd of unruly weavers would have stopped rioting immediately, apologised sincerely to Sir Philip Musgrave and his Tory companions, touched their forelocks and said things like "Sir, we are so very sorry for creating this disturbance. We will of course accompany you immediately to the jail." However, this was Real Life and not popular fiction, and the Mayor was not a Nineteenth Century version of Batman. The crowd of rioters grabbed the Mayor and the two constables and threw them in the mill pond to join Sir Philip and the rest of his cronies.

The Mayor managed to struggle out of the water and sent to the garrison at the Castle for help. A troop of armed soldiers duly arrived, but the rioting crowd then turned on them, hurling rocks and stones at them. As we have seen in the modern times, throwing stones at armed troops is not a sensible thing to do, but a crowd in full riot mode have usually left their common sense behind some time before. The troops fired their rifles over the heads of the crowd to try and quieten them down. Fortunately their shots missed the crowd, but unfortunately they hit a woman who was watching from an upstairs window and killed her.

This only increased the tension and over the next few days riots spread throughout the city. Word of the Carlisle riots came to the ears of Sir Robert Peel, the Home Secretary and the founder of the police force. Sir Robert wrote an angry letter to the Mayor of Carlisle demanding that steps be taken to bring Law and Order to Carlisle. The Mayor protested that he had been trying to do exactly that, but had been thrown in the mill pond by the mob for his trouble, and what else was he expected to do? But Sir Robert Peel was insistent: it was bad enough having Carlisle filled with warring Scots for the past few hundred years, but Rioting Weavers was a far more dangerous thing. Under pressure from the Home Secretary and the Government, Carlisle Corporation was reluctantly forced to spend money to set up a proper Police Force. This new Police Force consisted of four Constables and 14 Night Watchmen, and by 1857 this had increased to 34 police officers.

By the end of the Nineteenth Century, Carlisle's police force were finding their resources stretched as the city's expanding population was kept afloat by the city's breweries. Something had to be done to end the Drink Culture that dominated Carlisle ... and it was done in the most drastic way possible.

15 - DRINK AND GUNPOWDER: CARLISLE'S STATE-OWNED PUBS

As we saw in the last chapter, one thing that became apparent during the Carlisle of the Nineteenth Century was how large a part alcohol had played. It wasn't just the weavers who got drunk, it was their children as well. In fact almost everyone in Carlisle got drunk. This was because the water in the city at that time was so foul, and also so dangerous (the cause of typhoid, cholera, etc), that no-one drank it. Instead whole families drank ale.

They weren't the only ones. With the expansion of the railways in the Nineteenth Century came the men who built the railways, the navvies, thousands of them, mainly from Ireland. They worked hard, and their main relaxation after a week's hard work was drinking. And that didn't mean drinking the water in Carlisle, which they had heard was dangerous

Above: The Carlisle Arms or The Gaol Tap in its hey day.

to health. No, they preferred Strong Drink: especially beer and whisky, or anything with alcohol in it. And Carlisle, awash with breweries, was the place to provide solace for their thirsts.

In 1914 the Great War (later known as World War I) began. Britain and its Empire were in desperate need of weapons and ammunition and it was decided to build a munitions factory at Gretna, just 9 miles away from Carlisle. Not just any old factory, this was going to be the Biggest Munitions Factory in the whole of the British Empire, stretching miles along the north side of the Solway from Gretna to Eastriggs.

The men who built this enormous factory were the same sort of men who had built the railways: 10,000 navvies, many from Ireland, as had been the case with the navvies who built the railways.

In addition there were about 20,000 munitions workers, mainly women. A total of 30,000 people doing hard and thirsty work. The nearest pub was in Carlisle, and the only available train from Gretna to Carlisle on a working night arrived in Carlisle just five minutes before closing time.

For the munition workers and the navvies this was a serious situation, one they tried to solve in two ways: the first was to take a collection among the munition workers and navvies waiting for this train and use this money to bribe the engine driver to get into Carlisle faster than the timetable specified. With only five minutes to spare before closing time, every second counted.

The second solution was to come to an arrangement with the bars nearest to Carlisle station, one of which was Boustead's Bar, owned by Sammy Boustead. This arrangement meant that Sammy would line up the drinks all ready for the crowds as they rushed in through the doors soon after the train got in. There are reports of Sammy Boustead setting out five hundred glasses of whiskey ten minutes before closing time, ready for the nightly stampede.

The combination of hundreds, nay, thousands of workers rushing into the Carlisle pubs and pouring alcohol as fast as they could down their throats late at night meant that Carlisle soon gained a reputation similar to the Wild West towns of America as drunks lurched around the streets, either to commit mayhem or be robbed.

The respectable folk of Carlisle were shocked at what was

The Crescent Inn in Warwick Road, near to the Post Office. The Crescent Inn was just one of many pubs designed by the architect Harry Redfern during the years of State Management. It is a superb blend of Art Nouveau and Spanish-Moorish, wonderfully out of keeping with the rather drab run-of-the-mill architecture found in much of Carlisle during the early 20th Century. Harry's vision for Carlisle's pubs first took shape with his reworking of The Malt Shovel on the corner of Corporation Road, and others soon followed: The Apple Tree in Lowther Street, the Coach and Horses in Kingstown, the Magpie at Botcherby, and many others. But it as the Crescent Inn which is generally reckoned to be his crowning achievement. If only other Government Departments had allowed their public-owned buildings to be designed by similarly wild imaginations, how much more exotic life in Britain would be. Harry Redfern's lasting contribution to the pubs and drinkers of Carlisle is celebrated in The Redfern Inn on St Anne's Hill in Carlisle, which was designed by Harry Redfern's assistant, Joseph Seddon.

St Albans Row, still looking much the same in Victorian times as it does today.

happening in their city, and the religious leaders - especially those associated with the Temperance Movement - called for severe action to be taken to stop this drunkenness and lawlessness. Their concern was shared by the Minister for Munitions, David Lloyd George, but for different reasons. He realised that to have a load of drunks, or people with severe hangovers, handling explosives was not the best idea. With the Great War well under way there was a serious risk of the area around Carlisle being blown to smithereens by the workers and all the ammunition for the troops going up in smoke, along with Carlisle, Gretna and Eastriggs.

In an effort to stop mobs of thousands of drunks roaming around Carlisle on a weekend, the Magistrates banned the sale of alcohol on Sundays. This idea, which some bright spark had obviously worked hard

In Victorian and Edwardian times geese were brought by boat from Ireland to the port of Silloth, and were then walked all the way from Silloth to The Sands at Carlisle, a distance of 21 miles.

on, was seen to be completely crackpot on the very first weekend it came into force: the munition workers and navvies simply bought enough booze on a Saturday night to keep them going until Monday.

In desperation the authorities looked at the options open to them. One was prohibition, but there was a serious danger that this would lead to a rise in organised crime, with gangsters controlling illegal booze (as happened in America when prohibition was introduced there). There was also the more immediate risk of riots among the navvies and munition workers if they discovered that alcohol was banned.

There was another option, a very radical one indeed: if the Government couldn't stop the people drinking, then they would take over the pubs and try and control the levels of drink. And that is what happened. In 1916, as an experiment, the Central Control Board (Liquor Traffic) was set up and took over most of the pubs in Carlisle, including the Border Reiver, the Bush Inn, the Caledonian, the Crescent Inn, the Cumberland Wrestlers, the Jovial Sailor, the Maltsters Arms, and many many more.

And not just in Carlisle: the Central Control Board took over many of the pubs in towns and villages for many miles around Carlisle, including Aspatria, Wigton, Maryport, Kirkbride, Bothel, Port Carlisle, Bowness on Solway, Burgh by Sands.

It also bought off-licences and small shops with a licence to sell alcohol, as well as hotels and guests houses (although it left Carlisle's major hotels, The Crown and Mitre, the Station and the County alone as they didn't have public bars and so the navvies and munitions workers stayed away from them). As the piece-de-resistance the Government also bought the four privately-owned breweries in the city.

This was an early example of nationalisation, long before the Labour Government elected in 1945 brought in the Welfare State, long before the nationalisation of the health service, or the railways, and a year before the 1917 Bolshevik Revolution bought State Control of Absolutely Everything to Russia.

By October 1916 the majority of the pubs and off-licences in Carlisle were under the control of the Central Control Board.

One of the first rules laid down under the new Control Board was the rationing of drink: only one drink per person. Drinkers used to get round this by going to the bar and ordering a whole round of drinks for himself "and my friends", or "I'm treating my friends to a few drinks". The drinker would then stagger to a table under the weight of a tray of drinks, and consume the lot before any of these so-called friends turned up. As a result, a new law was brought in: "No Treating". Under this law it was now illegal for anyone to buy anyone else a drink.

And to make sure that these laws were not flouted, Drink Inspectors were appointed, whose job was to check on all places in Carlisle that sold alcohol. Any place that broke the rules could be closed down.

As we have seen, Lloyd George introduced this scheme because he was worried that the munition workers would drink too much and either blow themselves up or make a mess of the explosive mix and send out sub-standard ammunition to the troops. So, when the Great War ended in 1918 and the demand for explosives began to subside, most of the people in Carlisle assumed that the scheme would end and they could go back to the good old days of getting roaring drunk and committing mayhem and violence before throwing up all over the place and falling unconscious in pools of vomit. They were wrong.

Although the scheme had been set up as "an experiment" in 1916, the authorities must have decided that they hadn't got enough results yet to decide whether the experiment had worked, because although the Central Control Board was abolished in 1921, it was replaced by The Carlisle and District State Management Scheme, which carried on with exactly the same rules as before as far as the sale and consumption of alcohol was concerned. Most of the pubs in Carlisle remained under State control with rules and regulations regarding how much drink could be sold. And you still couldn't buy a round of drinks for friends, which was a very useful excuse for the miserly drinker.

State Management of most of the pubs in and around Carlisle remained in force until Reginald Maudling, the Home Secretary in the Conservative Government of 1971, decided that enough was enough: the experiment was over. Whether it smacked too much of nationalisation and the socialist State, or whether the Civil Service had got fed up with running Carlisle's pubs from Whitehall in London, is not known. What is known is that in 1971 the State control of Carlisle's drinking houses came to an end. In a word … Cheers!

Modern Carlisle. The Civic Centre and Eastern Way - two signs of progress that now look like mistakes.

16 - CHANGES

In his book, "Strong Lad Wanted For Strong Lass", the Carlisle-bred writer Hunter Davies describes Carlisle as "a dirty, dreary, noisy, smoky industrial town". This is not a man to argue with because: a) he is a very famous, talented and perceptive writer; and b) he lived there from 1940 until 1958. If Hunter Davies (still a strong champion of all things Cumbrian) says Carlisle was a dump during the 1940s and 50s, then it must have been. So when did it change? What happened to turn it from the sort of place that would have been the perfect location for any heart-rending dramatic film about life among the grinding poor, set in a grimy soot-stained city, where visitors say "By heck, it's grim up north" .. to the semi-cosmopolitan city it is today?

Some think the transition began during the 1930s. Lloyd George

Above: The Old Lanes are remembered with affection by many people. They were replaced after many years by a prize-winning shopping centre.

may have brought drinking in Carlisle under strict control with his 1916 legislation bringing in State management, but there was no doubt that many of the people in Carlisle lived in appalling conditions, drunk or sober. As we saw earlier, The Lanes in the centre of Carlisle was the sort of place that gave slums a bad name; and by the 1930s most of the houses in The Lanes were classed as being "unfit for human habitation". Large housing estates, like the Raffles Estate, were built away from the centre of Carlisle and many of the families who lived in The Lanes were moved to these estates.

With the centre of the city cleared of many of its inhabitants, the people of Carlisle assumed that the old decrepit buildings in The Lanes would be demolished and a whole new Carlisle City Centre would spring up in their place. As had been so often the case in the past, the people of Carlisle were wrong. In this case the problem was The Curse of The Committee . . . or, to be precise, Committees.

It is often said that about the only thing any Committee can agree on is the date of the next meeting . . . and even this is problematic. When it comes to reaching decisions about the actual business on the agenda, this can take years. Usually, by the time a decision is about to be reached, events have overtaken it. One UK Council took so long to approve the installation of a bus shelter on a rural bus route, that by the time the bus shelter was built and officially opened, the bus route had been discontinued.

The Carlisle Corporation and its various Committees of the early and mid-Twentieth Century were no exception to this rule of "Talk But Little Action". During the 1930s the debate carried on about what to do about The Lanes, and the whole centre of Carlisle. This debate was interrupted by the arrival of the Second World War in 1939, and then continued in 1945. By 1954 a scheme for partial rebuilding of the Lanes had been submitted, and rejected. After more meetings and more debate, by 1962 a decision had been taken to completely redevelop the area. As the 1970s drew to a close, with discussions still taking place about what to do with The Lanes and how to do it, nature - or, rather gravity - took a hand in the decision-making: many of the old derelict buildings collapsed. The resulting large hole in the centre of the city forced the local Corporation to Do Something, and during 1979 and 1980 the construction of the modern Lanes Shopping Centre was under way, which was officially opened in 1984.

Having been rather exhausted by this sudden rush of decision-making (it had only taken almost 40 years for them to resolve the situation), it is understandable that the City Corporation felt the need to recover before making further decisions about the centre of Carlisle. But when they did, it was another Big Decision . . . possibly even bigger than the one about developing The Lanes. The decision was made to Get Rid of Traffic In The City Centre, and so, in 1989, the cars and buses which had been so much a feature of mid-Twentieth Century Carlisle as they wound their way around the Cross and past the Old Town Hall were banished to a one-way system circumnavigating the city centre.

Almost overnight (or, at least in the space of 20 years, which is fast by North Cumbria standards) Carlisle city centre was transformed into the modern - and still developing - city we see today.

Paying homage to Hughie McIlmoyle, probably the finest player to grace a Carlisle shirt.

17 - CARLISLE UNITED

The emotional life of the majority of football supporters is hard. Only one team can win a Division, whether it's the Premiership, Championship, League One, League Two, the Conference or the Infant School and Kindergarten Division. Only one team can win the FA Cup. For every other team each season is one of disappointment, gloom and despair, interspersed with rejoicing over a victory, or your goalkeeper saving a penalty, or (in the case of Carlisle United's goalkeeper Jimmy Glass) scoring the goal that kept Carlisle in the Football League in 1999.) The emotional life of a Carlisle United supporter is no different to 99.9% of other football supporters on match day: agony and ecstasy on the terraces, or sitting at home listening to the match commentary on BBC Radio Cumbria and chewing the furniture in desperation.

Football in Cumbria began in earnest in 1884 with the formation of Workington FC, and in those early days Workington were The Top Dogs in the Beautiful Game in Cumbria. However, in the 1885/1886 season a team simply known as Carlisle played Workington in the Final of the Cumberland Cup on 27th March 1886 at Highmoor Park, Wigton. Carlisle won, 2-0. The next year the same two teams got through to the Final again, only this time Workington beat Carlisle 8-0.

Unfortunately, with the arrival of the Carlisle team's supporters came the first tragic instance of football hooliganism in Cumbria: in 1887 after Workington had beaten Carlisle in a game, Carlisle's supporters threw stones at the Workington players as they left the pitch. One of the Workington players, John Roberts Fisher, was so badly injured that he was taken to hospital. He was in a coma for twenty weeks, and then he died.

By the 1889/1890 season, the city of Carlisle boasted two rival football teams: Red Rose and Shaddongate United, and it was Shaddongate United that evolved into Carlisle United in 1904.

Carlisle United's first ground was Millholme Bank in Currock, but even by the standards of the time, Millholme Bank was more of a field with a shed on it than a proper football ground. Such was the poor state of this home ground that when the mighty Glasgow Rangers came to Carlisle to play United in April 1905, the match was played at the rugby ground in

Warwick Road. Whether it was the spectre of rugby that caused the Carlisle forwards to put a lot of their shots over the bar, or because they were unused to playing on a pitch not dotted with molehills, but Carlisle lost that match 2-1.

The last match Carlisle United played at Millholme was the Hospital Cup Final against their old rivals Red Rose, on 6th May 1905. During the season United had won the Senior League Championship and the Cumberland Cup, and had already beaten Red Rose in those competitions. As far as United's supporters were concerned Carlisle United were the absolute favourites to win the game by a country mile. Red Rose won 1-0.

In 1905 Carlisle United moved to Devonshire Park (now part of the playing fields at Newman School), and - with a run of wins - Carlisle United looked as if they were headed for the top. Unfortunately another topic surfaced, one that was to haunt Carlisle United throughout its history even to the 21st century: Money. In 1909, with huge debts, including owing large sums in back rent to their landlord, the Duke of Devonshire, Carlisle United were forced to leave Devonshire Park, and for a while it looked as if the club would fold altogether. The Duke did his best to help, writing off the back rent the club owed him, but more help was needed if the club was to survive. Help came in the form of supporters buying £1 shares in the club. This money went toward buying the present ground at Brunton Park off Warwick Road, and developing it into a proper football ground.

In 1928 Carlisle United entered the big time when they joined the Football League.

Carlisle's first few seasons in the Football League were not remarkable, except for the size of some of their defeats, including being defeated 8-1 in 1933 by Wrexham, and 6-1 by non-League side Wigan in the FA Cup in 1934. However, the Club persevered, and by the 1950s Carlisle could be proud of some of the footballers who wore their colours, especially the mighty Billy Hogan, described as possibly the best winger Carlisle ever had. Billy Hogan joined Carlisle from Manchester City in 1949, the same year as United got a new manager: the legendary Billy Shankly. Under Shankly, performances improved, and despite Shankly leaving Carlisle in 1951, things looked good for United. On Christmas

Day 1952 it was Carlisle's turn to be the high scorers, hammering 8 goals past Scunthorpe in an 8-0 victory.

With all the omens looking good, disaster struck. In March 1953 there was a fire during the night which completely destroyed the main stand at Brunton Park. Along with the stand went the club's equipment and its paper records. It is reckoned that the fire was started by a dropped cigarette end, left lying on the ground by a careless smoker after a game against Falkirk.

Faced with this disaster the Mayor of Carlisle, George Bowman, launched an appeal to raise money to build a new stand, with the football ground to be used as security for a loan. However, that appeal ground to a halt when potential investors found out that the football ground at Brunton Park was already being used as security for an overdraft.

Carlisle fans will be aware of echoes of these same financial problems for United in the 21st Century.

Fortunately for United, the Football Association loaned the club £4,000. The new Manager, Fred Emery, called a meeting of the different organisations that had been set up to raise funds for the club and urged them to work together. With the money these organisations jointly raised, plus the £4,000 loan from the Football Association, and £2,000 from the insurance money for the burnt-out stand, plus £12,000 from the sale of Carlisle player Geoff Twentyman to Liverpool, the money was found to get Carlisle United back on track.

In 1965 Chris Balderstone joined Carlisle from Huddersfield. Not only was he a superb footballer who became United's captain, but he was also an outstanding cricketer who played for Yorkshire and Leicestershire, a double talent which caused him problems when the cricket and football seasons coincided. In 1973 Balderstone chose to finish playing out the cricket season, which meant missing United's opening games. As a result he lost the captaincy of the club. However, by the end of the season, with Balderstone playing a key role once he had hung up his cricket bat and pads, Carlisle United had gained something much greater . . . promotion to the First Division. In August 1974 Carlisle achieved the unbelievable, they topped the First Division!

Alas, that was to be the pinnacle of achievement for United. By 1975 they were back in Division 2, and by 1977 back in Division 3.

During the early 1980s United see-sawed between Divisions 2 and 3, and from 1987 they joined Division 4. In 1992 United were back in Division 3, but only because the name of Division 4 was changed to Division 3.

It was once famously said: "Some people say that football's a matter of life and death .. well it's much more important than that." For supporters of Carlisle United every season is a matter of life and death, each and every game a cause of potential heart attacks among so many of their supporters. This was never the case more so than during the 2003/2004 season, because in 2004 Carlisle United celebrated the 100th anniversary of their formation in the most miserable fashion possible: after season after season of hanging on by their shinpads in the League, they were relegated to the Conference.

With Workington Town and Barrow having been relegated from the League many years before, for the first time ever the county of Cumbria had no team in the Football League.

Fortunately for Carlisle's supporters, after just one nail-biting season in the Conference, United returned to League Two (previously known as Division 3) in 2005. At the time of writing their progress in League Two is an echo of their progress over the previous 100 years: a game of snakes and ladders ... this time they're going up another ladder.

18 - THE FLOODS AND THE FUTURE

On the night of 7th January 2005 severe storms battered Cumbria, bringing down power lines and leaving many parts of the county without electricity. The Spring tides rushed in from the sea, overwhelming the rivers that ran through the city of Carlisle. A Spring tide is a powerful force of nature, a wall of water hurtling forward at 30 to 40 miles an hour.

For Carlisle the combination of storm damage, the high tides, and storm water filling up all the drains brought disaster. As dawn rose on Saturday 8 January 2005, Carlisle city centre was flooded, in places up to ten feet deep. All traffic lights were out of action. Not that there was any place for cars to go, the only form of transport that could move through the streets of central Carlisle were small boats.

Most Cumbrians - at least those with batteries to power their radios - tuned in to BBC Radio Cumbria and listened to the reports of the damage, and the weather forecast. The forecast didn't look good. More heavy rain was expected.

Above: A car negotiates the flood s in Caldewgate. in 1925.

115

The houses along Warwick Road, the main thoroughfare from Carlisle to the east and to the M6 Motorway, were devastated, as were the side roads leading off Warwick Road, with people trapped in the upstairs of the houses having to be rescued by boats, by the Coastguard, the police, the fire services, and by anyone who happened to have a boat they could launch. The problem was that it is one thing to navigate a boat along a river, it is quite another to try and navigate along a road aware that cars, motorbikes, signs and bollards are just below the surface of the dark sewage-filled waters and could tear a hole in the bottom of that boat at any moment; especially when the boat is a RIB (Rigid Inflatable Boat), the type used by the Coastguard. From experience, I know this only too well, having served as a volunteer for a year with this same Coastguard crew. (As an aside: after the floods, when Awards were being handed out for bravery and civic actions, it was a surprise to discover that many people, including those in authority in the city, weren't aware that the Coastguard crew are all volunteers and not an official paid emergency service.)

Private individuals joined the rescue: Wigton solicitor John Hawks heard the appeal for boat-owners on the local radio, and set off for Carlisle

Willowholme and Brunton Park Avenue (opposite) were no longer suitable for motor vehicles.

with his 16foot motorboat on tow. Reaching Carlisle at 9am, he launched his boat in Caldewgate and for the rest of the day worked with other volunteers to rescue more than 80 people. One of his most difficult rescues was that of an elderly woman who had a broken leg. Firemen got into her house and tore the door off her wardrobe to use as a makeshift stretcher, and then loaded her into John's boat.

Another hero was Darren Brown, who spent almost 10 hours in the polluted chest-deep freezing water hauling his small boat behind him as he went from house to house, taking people out of their houses through their windows.

These are just examples of the physical courage and help that was shown on that day as people helped strangers they had never known before, because the community worked together.

Another hero of the day was Martin Plenderleith, presenter on BBC

Radio Cumbria. Martin had turned up at 5.15 am to present his morning breakfast show. He was still at BBC Radio Cumbria that evening, still broadcasting, trapped in the building by the floodwaters. No-one else could get in to the building through the floods, and no-one could get out. The mains electricity had failed, as it had across Carlisle, and the radio station was being powered by a back-up generator. With reduced lighting, no food except snacks from a vending machine, no computers to keep him informed on events but just a landline phone to hand, Martin and his producer, Steve Urqhart kept the show on the air for a marathon 12 hours, keeping people informed with what was happening, helping direct the emergency services and the rescuers to where they were needed. It has to be remembered that all the houses affected were without electricity, and in January the weather is cold and daylight is very short. Martin's calm tones (if rather hoarse by 5pm) kept the spirits of the people up, let them know that things would be alright if they just kept calm, and kept in touch with one another through him.

Even though the rains came again, and it was days before power was restored to many parts of the area, the people of Carlisle came through. Sadly, three people died in the floods, but the death toll would have been much higher without the rescuers, both professional and voluntary.

After the waters had subsided the overall picture could finally be seen, and the cost counted. Businesses were wiped out . . . some for ever. Some businesses forced to close by the flood water have never re-opened, the damage to their premises was far too great. Some found it impossible to get insurance in the future. People lost their homes and their possessions. Not just practical things like washing machines and furniture, but things that could never be replaced: emotional souvenirs: photographs, family keepsakes, letters, diaries, all destroyed in one night of flood. At the time of writing (winter 2005) the houses on both sides of Warwick Road and the neighbouring streets around still look like building sites. Nearly a year on and many families are still unable to get back into their homes. But the people of Carlisle have endured 2,000 years of tribulations: wars, siege, plague, fire . . . and now flood. As a Cumbrian said to me as he looked at his wrecked house in the centre of Carlisle: "Ah well. Move on. No sense in twining."

And that is the strength of the people of Carlisle. There's no sense in twining. Look to the future.

And what of the future?

As the 21st Century unfolds, Carlisle is changing as a city. Botchergate, once thought of as a no-go area except for prostitutes and muggers, has been torn down and become an upmarket entertainment area, with a modern multiplex cinema, hotel, food venues, cafes, bars.

The houses that made up Lanes, once one of the biggest slums in Carlisle, were replaced by a large modern Shopping Centre, still retaining the name The Lanes.

In 2007 it is intended that Carlisle will be the main campus for a new University of Cumbria.

A Western bypass linking the main western routes out of the city with Junction 44 of the M6 is planned to try and stop the gridlock in the centre of the city.

But these are cosmetic changes. The heart of Carlisle lies in the people of Carlisle. Their wishes, their hopes, their dreams, their daily lives.

For nearly 2,000 years, ever since the Romans arrived and decided that the high point overlooking the Eden, the Petterill and the Caldew rivers would make a good position for a fort, Carlisle has expanded: from a fort, to a castle, to a town, to a city. A city with a turbulent history, a city whose people have suffered over the centuries from war, fire, famine, plague and siege. But the people of Carlisle not only suffered, they survived, and they have triumphed. In these early years of the 21st Century the future for Carlisle looks bright. It is the people of Carlisle who are writing the city's history as they go about their daily lives, a history which will be told in future days long hence. And when it is written, perhaps that writer will also begin their tale with Carlisle, the Camp of Lug, the Heart of the Borders.

CARLISLE TIMELINE

4000BC - Middle Stone Age (Mesolithic Era): small groups, cleared forests and hunted game.
New Stone Age (Neolithic era): New settlers arrived. Stone axes and other tools. Farming.

2000BC - Bronze Age: Round houses (found on site of The Lanes). Brigante tribe settle.

AD72: Romans arrive. Construct fort.

AD83: Roman garrison at Carlisle increases in size.

AD122: Hadrian's Wall begins construction.

AD330-340: Roman fort at Carlisle abandoned by the military.

AD685: St Cuthbert, Bishop of Lindisfarne, comes to Carlisle.

AD867: Vikings arrive and lay waste to Carlisle.

1092: William II (William Rufus) arrives in Carlisle. Orders construction of fort.

1122: Henry I comes to Carlisle, orders construction of more substantial castle.
Foundation of Augustinian priory.

1158: Henry II gives Town Charter to Carlisle.

1174: Carlisle under siege by King William the Lion of Scotland.

1216: Carlisle taken by King Alexander of Scotland.

1233: Two groups of friars arrive to set up monasteries: The Franciscans (also known a Greyfriars) begin building in the area between Bank Street and Devonshire Street.
The Dominicans (or Blackfriars) at first settle outside the city walls in Botchergate.

1237: The border between England and Scotland defined at the Treaty of

York. Carlisle officially part of England.

1238: Dominicans move to permanent site in Blackfriars Street.

1251: Fire destroys large parts of Carlisle.

1292 A major fire destroys much of the walled town, including the cathedral, the bridge of the castle, the Franciscan friary, and parts of the Dominican friary, as well as many houses and warehouses and orchards.

1297: William "Braveheart" Wallace launches an attack against Carlisle.

1307: Edward I dies at Burgh-by-Sands.

1349: The Black Death comes to Carlisle, killing two thirds of the population.

1391: Fire destroys three quarters of Carlisle.

1402: Scots attack Carlisle.

1430: Carlisle struck by plague.

1456: War between England and Scotland begins. Carlisle attacked by Scots.

1541: Dissolution of the Monasteries by Henry VIII leads to closure of Carlisle Priory.

1545: The two towers of the Courts built for defence of Carlisle.

1568: Mary Queen of Scots imprisoned in Carlisle Castle.

1596: The Border Reiver, Kinmont Willie, freed from Carlisle Castle.

1644 - 1645: Siege of Carlisle by Parliament Forces.

1715: Jacobite forces under James Edward (James III) attack Carlisle area.

1745: Jacobite forces under Bonnie Prince Charlie invade Carlisle.

1800s: Industrial revolution: textile industry dominates Carlisle.

1823: Canal between Carlisle and Solway Firth opens.

1826: Riot in Carlisle during Election.

1837: Carlisle and Newcastle Railway opens.

1845: Carlisle - Maryport Railway opens.

1848: Citadel Railway station opens.

1904: Carlisle United FC formed.

1916: Central Control Board brings pubs in Carlisle and surrounding area under State control.

1971: End of State Control of Carlisle pubs.

1980: "The Lanes" residential area demolished and replaced with The Lanes Shopping Centre.

2005: Major floods in Carlisle.

Further Reading

Carlisle's interesting and exciting history has been the subject of many books, although there has never been a thoroughgoing and authoritive history of the city.

The best place to start is Denis Perriam's *Carlisle: An Illustrated History*. The story is told thematically with sections on the City Mills, Non-conformist Chapels, Banks, and Victoria Viaduct as well the obvious things like the Cathedral and the Castle.

Denis Perriam is also reponsible for several collections of old photographs of the city: *Carlisle in Camera: Volumes One and Two; Images of England: Carlisle; and Carlisle Remembered*.

Denis has been writing weekly articles on local history for *The Cumberland News* for many years. They are a superb source for details of all aspects of Carlisle's past.

A similar set of articles were written by James Walter Brown in the earlier part of the twentieth century. The best of these were collected into nine volumes called *Round Carlisle Cross*. Further anecdotes from the city's history are to be found in *Memories of Old Carlisle by Two Carel Lads,* George Topping and John Potter.

The classic history of the city, *Carlisle* in *The Historic Towns* series was written by the eminent Victorian historian Mandell Creighton. Creighton was born in Castle Street, Carlisle.

Another general history was written by Joyce and Brian Blake. Their book, *The Story of Carlisle,* is a good popular account of the city and was presented to many schoolchildren in the fifties.

There have been other modern histories by Mike McCarthy and Sidney Towill.

One of the finest of scholarly local history books is Henry Summerson's *Mediaeval Carlisle*. It treats the history of the city in exhaustive detail and is written with great clarity and enthusiasm.

Mike McCarthy was, for many years, the City Archaeologist, and he has been reponsible for some fine scholarly volumes on the various digs in the city including the extensive work done prior to the building of the new Lanes Shopping Centre.

The book Mike edited on the history of *Carlisle Castle* is exhaustive in its treatment of one of the most historically interesting castles in the country.

Canon David Weston has written an equally comprehensive account of *Carlisle Cathedral*.

David Ramshaw and Denis Perriam have produced a splendid pictorial survey of the *Citadel Railway Station* and David Ramshaw has also written an attractive book on *The Carlisle Canal*. Peter W. Robinson has written of Carlisle's important role in railway history in *Rail Centres: Carlisle*.

Perhaps the most enthralling book on Carlisle's history has been Margaret Forster's *Rich Desserts and Captain's Thin* which tells the story of the Carr family and the growth of their biscuit making business. Many of Margaret Forster's novels are set in Carlisle and together they offer a very special picture of the city's recent social history.

Margaret's husband, Hunter Davies, has written an entertaining account of his early years growing up in Carlisle called *Strong Lad Wanted for Strong Lass,* and his novel *Here We Go Round the Mulberry Bush* was set in 1950s Carlisle.

Many detailed articles on individual aspects of Carlisle's history are to be found in the *Transactions of the Cumberland and Westmorland Antiquarian and Archaeological Society* which have been published annually since 1874.

For people interested in family trees, Carlisle and Cumberland have been well covered by a series of nineteenth century *Directories* which began with Jollie's which was published in Carlisle in 1811 and includes others published by Jefferson, Mannix and Whellan and Bulmer.

The Lanes Library in Carlisle contains an excellent local history collection and the County Archives, housed in Carlisle Castle, are well worth a visit.

All books currently in print can be obtained from Bookends, 56 Castle Street, Carlisle, (01228 529067) or from www.bookscumbria.com. Out of print books are often available from Bookcase, 19 Castle Street, Carlisle. (01228 544560) Bookcase is one of the largest second-hand bookshops in the country and keeps a very large stock of local books.

Books Published by Bookcase

Strong Lad Wanted For Strong Lass: Growing Up In Carlisle Hunter Davies £8.99
Hunter Davies is one of the country's best known writers and journalists, author of over 30 books. This is his fascinating personal story of growing up in Carlisle in the 1950's.

A New Illustrated History of Wigton   John Higham   £11.50
A detailed, well-researched history spanning nearly two thousand years of this small market town. Covers some sixty five topics and includes about 275 illustrations, many never previously published.

Cumberland and Westmorland Wrestling.   Roger Robson   £8.95
A modern history of Cumberland and Westmorland wrestling.

Border Television: A History.   Mary Scott Parker.   £7.95
A collection of personal memories from the local broadcasters who have been involved in the television station over the years.

A Border Naturalist: The Birds & Wildlife of the Bewcastle Fells & the Gilsland Moors, 1930 - 1966   Ritson Graham   £10.00
A beautifully written study of the rich and varied wildlife in one of the last unspoilt areas of the country.

The Antique County Maps of Cumberland   John Higham.   £11.99
The lavishly illustrated story of the printed maps of Cumberland.

The Anatomy of the Helm Wind.   David Uttley.   £9.95
A unique study which examines the only named wind in Britain.

Beatys Illustrated Guide to Carlisle   £2.95
A facsimile reprint of the original guide from 1905, first designed to show the Edwardian tourist the finer sights of the flourishing Border city.

A History of Alston Moor.   Alistair Robertson.   £8.95
The first history of the highest market town In England, the story of a people and their landscape throughout the centuries.

The Changing Face of Brampton.   Iain Parsons.   £11.50
Over 150 rare photos and a detailed, informative text display the author's affection for the area.

Provincial Pleasures.   Norman Nicholson.   £7.00
An affectionate tribute to the sturdy tradition of the Millom area.

History of Penrith. Ewanian (William Furness)   £7.50
A facsimile reprint of the original edition of 1894, giving a thorough history of Penrith and district up to the end of the nineteenth century.
The Black Angel.   Colin Bardgett.   £8.95
A valuable military record providing a fascinating insight into local history. The author has assembled diaries and letters written by men of the Penrith Volunteer Company.
Silloth. Mary Scott-Parker.   £8.95
A nostalgic history of this charming Victorian seaside town.
The History of Wigton. Thomas W. Carrick.   £8.95
A facsimile reprint of Carrick's famous work
Cockermouth Mechanics' Band.   Geoff Hunter.   £7.99
A history of the oldest band in Cumberland, richly illustrated throughout.
The Ghosts of Cumbria. Laurie Kemp.   £6.99
Laurie Kemp has ventured fearlessly among the lakes and fells to uncover the stories of the uneasy spirits that lurk in dark and eerie houses. . . .
The Loving Eye and Skilful Hand: The Keswick School of Industrial Arts.   Ian Bruce.   £15.00
This is the first detailed study of the Keswick School. It will be of interest to local and art historians and collectors.
Forty Years On: Carlisle and County High School for Girls 1884 - 1970. Mary Scott-Parker.   £7.95
An affectionate tribute to the High School. With archive photographs dating back to 1887. Introduced by Margaret Forster, a former pupil.
Hurry, Hurry, While Stocks Last. Hunter Davies.   £7.95
A sideways look at the economic, social and shopping history of Cumbria as seen through local advertisements 1850-1940. Hunter Davies traces the changes in Cumbrian life, in attitudes and activities, trends and fashions.
A Year At Ambleside: Harriet Martineau At Ambleside   Harriet Martineau; Barbara Todd   £10.00
Includes the first UK publication of A Year at Ambleside *by Harriet Martineau.*
The Carlisle Floods: One Story. Martin Daley.   £7.99
After the great Carlisle flood of January 2005 Martin and Wendy Daley had to watch day by day as their home was taken apart and then reconstructed.

Gretna's Secret War. Gordon L. Routledge. £7.95
In 1915 the greatest munitions factory on Earth was built at Gretna.
Carlisle Cathedral History. David W.V. Weston £14.95
The first detailed account of how the cathedral buildings have developed and changed over the centuries.
Longtown. Gordon L. Routledge. £11.95
Longtown, the last town in England, was an important crossing point on the River Esk on the border between Scotland and England. It was developed by the Grahams of Netherby and became a thriving market.
Carlisle and its Villages. Vincent White. £11.95
Vincent White began drawing the buildings of Carlisle as he saw familiar sights being demolished before his eyes.
Murder in Cumbria. Ian Ashbridge. £8.95
Ian Ashbridge researches the murders that took place in the beautiful county of Cumbria in the twentieth century.
Keswick: The Story of a Lake District Town. George Bott. £15
This elegant history tells the story of Keswick from the time of Castlerigg Stone Circle to the present day. Keswick has an importance far beyond its size. German miners came in Elizabethan times, the pencil was discovered here, it was a key centre of the Romantic revolution and later the town became famous for the Keswick Convention.